Have you wondered why the Chinese patrons in your favorite Chinese restaurant seem to be eating food that is not on your menu? As you probably suspected, the Chinese-language bill of fare is totally different from your English-language version. A wide gulf exists between the true Chinese food and the standard "Chinese-American" cuisine served in most restaurants.

The idea for this book emerged over a long period of time during which the author escorted groups of people to Chinese restaurants and ordered dinners for them in Chinese fashion, that is, by writing in Chinese. On many occasions she wondered how anyone who did *not* read Chinese might order the same authentic dishes. This guide is her answer.

The Scrutable Feast effectively removes the language barrier to great Chinese dining, allowing the reader to order true Chinese cuisine without knowing a single word of Chinese. Just take this book to your favorite Chinese restaurant. Then, make your choices from the English descriptions in the book and indicate them to the waiter by pointing to the Chinese characters beside each dish. Simply by pointing to the Chinese characters you can obtain the finest and most varied selection available in any Chinese restaurant anywhere in the world, from San Francisco and Vancouver to New York, London, or Paris.

The ideograms on the title page
and on the back of the jacket
are a familiar Chinese saying,
"Eating is the sky."

THE
SCRUTABLE
FEAST

═══●═══●═══●═══

A Guide

to Eating Authentically

in Chinese Restaurants

— dorothy farris lapidus —

DODD, MEAD & COMPANY   **NEW YORK**

Library of Congress Cataloging in Publication Data
Lapidus, Dorothy Farris.
   The scrutable feast.
   Includes index.
   1. Cookery, Chinese. 2. Gastronomy.
3. Food—Dictionaries—Chinese. I. Title.
TX641.L36   641.3   77–23429
ISBN 0–396–07448–0

This book is dedicated to Lucy, who once ate a half pound of black bean sauce all by herself.

My grateful thanks to Doris Safie for her assistance in researching the material for this book, and for her constant support and encouragement; to Lie-Won Woo Mook, Sarah Mook, Marcella Chin Dear, Yau Kwan Pak Le, and Teddy Lum for their invaluable aid in answering questions concerning Chinese cooking and the Chinese language; and to Richard Wong for his fine caligraphy. A special acknowledgment is extended to the late Ting-Yee Kuo of Columbia University for his help.

I am grateful to William Whipple, my editor, for his patience, sense of humor, and many good suggestions, and to my husband, Leonard, for his excellent constructive comments.

Particular thanks to Marilyn Tell Macksoud for typing this difficult manuscript, and almost losing a race with the stork in an effort to complete it. My gratitude to Betty Therriault for the final typing work, and for collating the completed manuscript.

Contents

Introduction

One of the things that is probably not needed at the present time is a new Chinese cookbook, and I have obliged by not writing one. This is a book about ordering and enjoying great Chinese food, not one about preparing it. Many excellent Chinese cookbooks have helped familiarize the Westerner with the exotic foodstuffs of the Orient, thus narrowing an ancient breach between East and West. Though the breach has been narrowed, however, it has not been bridged. The time and energy spent in preparing Chinese food at home does not perceptibly increase one's expertise in *ordering* authentic Chinese cuisine. Though many of my Western aquaintances are formidably skilled in the ways of the Chinese kitchen, they are still confronted with the great language barrier when they go to a Chinese restaurant. Only persons who can read Chinese or who have Chinese friends are really privy to what is, in my opinion, the finest cuisine in the world.

The purpose of this guide is to enable the reader to go into a Chinese restaurant and enjoy absolutely authentic Chinese food without knowing or using a single Chinese word. In the sections titled "The Cantonese Menu" and "The Szechwan Menu" are listed most of the dishes of Cantonese origin and of what is popularly called Szechwan cuisine that appear on standard Chinese menus. The names of the dishes are written in Chinese characters, the way they would appear on a Chinese menu, along with a translation and description of the dish. If the reader knows English and the waiter reads Chinese, it is possible with the use of this book to obtain the finest and most varied selection of Chinese dishes available in any Chinese restaurant by merely pointing to the characters. Of course, this is easier to do in Chinese restaurants in large cities and in Chinese-populated areas of these cities than in other areas, since the ingredients are more readily available there. But even when the guide is used in Chinese restaurants in smaller towns, the food that will be served will almost invariably be better and closer to real Chinese food than that served to other non-Chinese customers. Once while traveling through Ontario I stopped at a small Chinese restaurant where I observed some positively abysmal-looking food being served. I ordered a few basic dishes by writing their names in Chinese (the guide had not yet been written), and when the food was ready I was invited to dine with the family of the owner at their table. The food, although simple, unpretentious fare, was far better than anything the other customers were eating.

For the past several years I have accompanied groups of people to Chinese restaurants where, by writing in Chinese, I have ordered dinners coordinated to their tastes. This was possible because I had studied Chinese and had learned the Chinese menu, whose intricacies make it an entity apart from language. On many occasions friends would ask me to write in Chinese the names of the dishes I had ordered, so they could use them as future "model dinners" by just handing them to the waiter. One of my acquaintances made several copies of her four-dish dinner and distributed them among her friends who frequented Chinatown. I often wondered if any of the waiters thought it strange that so many Westerners were giving them little pieces of paper showing identical dishes. As amusing as it was to imagine these wrinkled paper scraps turning up in Chinatown kitchens, the incident did point up one very important fact: People are eager to experience the delights of Chinese food if they have the opportunity, but this opportunity can be provided only if the language barrier is overcome. I hope this book will make that possible and, in so doing, close the breach between true gourmets and the undiscovered feast that is Chinese food in America.

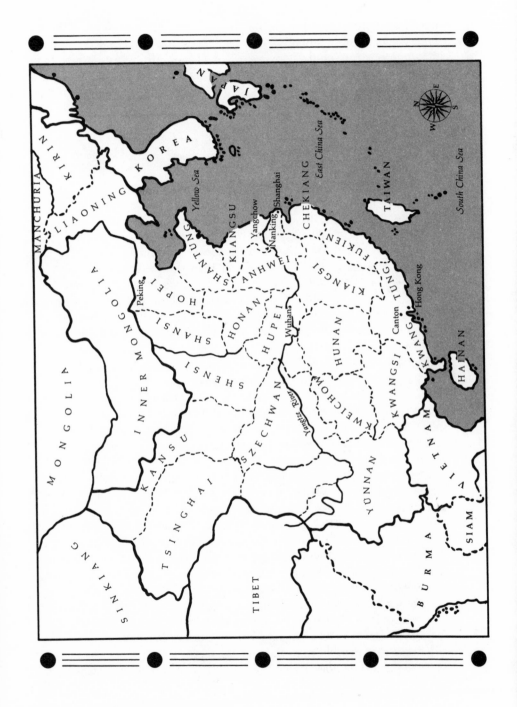

1

cHiNESE food iN AMERiCA:
tHE uNdiscoVEREd fEAst

During the past decade a growing interest in foreign cuisines has made Americans more familiar with heretofore exotic foods and more willing to experiment in restaurants and in their own kitchens. But if the general awareness of the culinary artistry of other lands has increased, the attention given to Chinese food alone, particularly within the past five years, is nothing short of phenomenal.

Travelers in the United States have no doubt come across the nearly ubiquitous Chinese restaurant during their journeys. Chinese restaurants are found not only in large or middle-sized cities, but even in the smallest of towns, where they have adapted to local tastes and tradition. I recall one such place in a tiny Western town where the chef, although Chinese, was undoubtedly influenced by the Spanish customs of the area, and so served a side dish of refried beans with whatever other food was ordered. Despite the seeming prevalence of such infractions throughout the American hinterlands and even in many large cities, it still can safely be asserted that the palate of the Chinese restaurant habitué is fast becoming so sophisticated that the "Column

A and Column B" individual may disappear altogether. Many dishes of the major cuisines of China are currently so familiar through various cooking courses and scores of cookbooks, and are available in so many good restaurants, at least in larger cities, as to offer us an embarrassment of riches. A further convenience to amateur chefs are such items as fresh ginger root, *bok choy*, mustard greens, and bean curd, which can now be purchased at many neighborhood markets.

Notwithstanding the relative ease of shopping and dining, most Americans are still denied the "total experience" of Chinese cuisine by their inability to read and understand the Chinese-language menu. Restaurants that cater to a sizable Chinese clientele distribute two differently colored menus to their patrons: one written in Chinese for Chinese customers, and one in English for all others. The fact that the English menu is not really a counterpart of the Chinese becomes clear when the non-Chinese patron tries to identify the dishes ordered by Chinese patrons and discovers they are not at all familiar. One reason for this disparity lies in the complexity of the Chinese language, which makes direct translation a cumbersome if not formidable task. Chinese syntax employs no tense, relative pronouns, or articles; moreover, a single ideograph, designating one syllable in Chinese, may require a multisyllabic word to translate it into English. These peculiarities contribute to an economy of space on the Chinese menu that is not possible on the English version.

Another factor to consider is that many Chinese vegetables and flavorings have no simple equivalents in English, thus requiring lengthy descriptions for any semblance of accuracy in translation. And the Chinese menu's use of fanciful or poetic expressions, with which the language is imbued, would confound readers even more, since they must recognize these gastronomic idioms as well. Of course, such idioms are important to any restaurant-goer regardless of language. What must the non-American think when confronted with "hot dog," "deviled eggs," and "baked Alaska"? And what of the unfortunate American in France whose conversational French may be quite good but whose menu vocabulary is inadequate? Such terms as *sole bonne femme*, *purée mongole*, and *rapée Morvandelle* could produce some rather bizarre images.

All this is by way of saying that those people who can read and understand the Chinese-language menu have an incomparable advantage over those who cannot. Not only are they able to choose from a much greater selection of dishes, but the dishes that are ordered will not be Anglicized. Interestingly, even American-born Chinese who speak the language are restricted in their selection if they are not able to read the Chinese menu. They may have more practical familiarity with the dishes than other Americans, but if they must order only from memory, their choices are limited.

This guide, therefore, is a translation and explanation of most of the dishes found on the Chinese-language menus that are generally used by Cantonese and Szechwan restaurants. (Noodle dishes, banquet fare, and certain "house specialties" have been excluded.) Cantonese and Szechwan cuisines were chosen because they are the two that are best known to Americans. Although restaurants designated as "Szechwan" usually serve dishes of Shanghai, Hunan, and Peking origin as well as those of Szechwan, they are still referred to as Szechwan-style restaurants.

Ordering from a Szechwan menu admittedly poses fewer problems for non-Chinese than ordering from a Cantonese menu. In a Szechwan restaurant, Chinese and non-Chinese patrons are given similar menus. Names of the dishes, which hardly ever exceed one hundred in number, are written in Chinese characters horizontally from left to right, with their translations next to the characters. A section written in Chinese, but untranslated, is sometimes included for Chinese patrons. Although the translations enable the non-Chinese patron to dine well and rather authentically, they are neither complete nor very accurate. Many excellent dishes are often deleted from Szechwan menus because of this communication gap, and are replaced by some all too familiar Chinese-American selections.

In contrast to the relative simplicity of the Szechwan menu, a Cantonese menu may list as many as 350 dishes, most of which are unknown to non-Chinese regardless of their level of gastronomic education. In Cantonese restaurants the English menu is abbreviated to 75 or 85 dishes that are largely ersatz Chinese. For example, "Shrimp with Lobster Sauce" is not a Chinese dish, but one that has been adapted to American preference. Often dishes having the same names as those on the Chinese menu are of questionable authenticity, since the method of preparation is frequently adjusted to what is generally assumed to be Western taste. The dark-brown soy-soaked fried rice on the English-language menu, for instance, has little in common with the light-colored, delicate dish bearing the same name on the Chinese menu, and which is eaten by the Chinese at the end of a banquet.

The number of dishes on the English menus of Chinese restaurants and the degree of their authenticity are largely matters of agreement between proprietors and patrons. The owner or chef will often prepare a menu based upon the menus of other restaurants with similar non-Chinese clienteles. Although the English-language menus of both Szechwan and Cantonese restaurants tend to be standardized, occasional variations occur if demand is great enough. Additions generally depend upon the Westerner's familiarity with the ingredients and preparation of various dishes. Deletions are often made because the translation of a particular item seems unclear or unappetizing to the diners, or because certain flavors or ingredients in a dish prove to be too exotic for them.

Such variations are much less likely to be found on Cantonese menus than on Szechwan. The typical English menus of Cantonese restaurants have remained very much the same for several decades. Their carbon-copy sameness probably resulted from a progression of trials and rejects. Communication barriers have tended to reinforce the status quo, and Cantonese restaurateurs are reluctant to change the pattern since experience has taught them that when a Westerner asks for "something really different," he will very often send it back to the kitchen because he doesn't like it. Obviously, to persist in offering "something different" is not economically feasible.

It is of sociological interest to note that even though people of Kwangtung province (whom we refer to as Cantonese) were the first Chinese to come to the United States in significant numbers, their communication problems vis-à-vis Westerners are still much more acute than those of other regional Chinese populations that immigrated later. The reasons for this difficulty become at least partially clear when the outlines of their early history in America are sketched in.

Like other immigrant groups, the first Cantonese in the United States clustered together, forming Chinatowns within the cities and towns where they found work. These communities grew to be so self-sufficient that commingling with the surrounding and often hostile Western culture became irrelevant to survival. Little or no effort was made to learn much English since it was unnecessary, and the improbability of communicating with Westerners in the difficult Cantonese dialect served to increase the insularity of the Cantonese population even more—an insularity that eventually would make it impossible to satisfy the curiosity of American restaurant-goers who wanted to know what it was they were eating.

Inasmuch as they brought to the New World a tradition of one of the finest and certainly the most diversified cuisines of all the provinces of China, it seems fitting that many enterprising Cantonese people opened restaurants. These early establishments, however, had little in common with even the most frugally equipped Cantonese restaurants of today. Native American produce, joined to Cantonese-style cooking, spawned that Chinese chicanery called "chop suey," as well as many other make-do dishes that pseudo-elitists of Chinese gastronomy would one day use to impugn the name of true Cantonese cuisine. But make-do or not, Americans fancied the new food. As the Chinese started to grow some of their native vegetables, the variety of dishes offered in their restaurants increased. Bean sprouts, snow peas, and some form of Chinese cabbage were surely introduced to Americans quite early, but the length of time that passed before they were widely accepted is unknown. During that period of adjustment, however, a sociological barrier was erected; a barrier due in part, perhaps, to the unfavorable reaction of American taste buds to many of the alien vegetables and seasonings.

By the time Chinese from other provinces immigrated to America, the Cantonese population here was already established in tightly knit communities. The old Chinatowns did not welcome any intrusion into what was regarded as Cantonese domain. Thus, although many of the later Chinese also opened restaurants, these were rarely or never within the Chinatowns' environs. Most of these newer dining places followed the Cantonese-style menu, since Americans were insufficiently familiar with other Chinese cuisines to warrant much digression from the beaten path. The first Chinese restaurants in America that were distinguishable from the ordinary Cantonese-American variety were those that described themselves as "Shanghai," "Peking," or "Mandarin," the last being a meaningless term when applied to food. While most of these restaurants still included Cantonese dishes, they featured dishes of other provinces as well. Nevertheless, the menu was written entirely in English, and Chinese patrons, if there were any, still ordered from a Chinese-language menu.

One cannot, with any great degree of certainty, tally all the events that led to the Sinicization of the American palate. But whatever sparked the development, a plethora of "different" Chinese restaurants began to appear within a relatively short period. Most of these identified themselves as Szechwan, but their menus frequently represented other regions of China as well. These restaurants achieved tremendous popularity rather quickly. The hot, spicy concoctions were a welcome change from the pleasant but nondescript flavors of the dishes usually consumed by Westerners in Cantonese restaurants. Moreover, the menus appeared to be authentic, since they were written in Chinese as well as in English. Finally, although Szechwan cuisine is intrinsically much more limited than true Cantonese cuisine, the menus of these new Szechwan restaurants far surpassed the stereotyped English menus in Cantonese dining places.

THE REGIONAL CUISINES OF CHINA

Although the menus translated and described in this guide are the Cantonese and Szechwan, many of the dishes included on these menus are regional fare of other provinces. Knowing something of the various cuisines of China and of the geographical regions that have spawned them is both interesting and useful. It must be emphasized, however, that neither styles of cooking nor their geographical boundaries have been unequivocally defined even by the cognoscenti. Some cookbook authors use simple compass-point designations, such as northern and southern cuisine, while others identify specific provinces or cities as the leading exponents of certain styles.

Both Westerners and Chinese have misconceptions about the geographical locations of many of China's cities and provinces. The terms "north" and "south" are used in much the same way that American city dwellers use "uptown" and "downtown." Both sets of directions depend upon one's point of reference. To the Cantonese, whose province of Kwangtung is the farthest south, all other provinces with their indigenous cooking are generally called "northern." To people from Peking, only Manchuria and Kirin are "northern"; most other provinces or cities and their regional food are referred to as "southern." It is therefore understandable that Westerners should be confused by Chinese geography. Most of us have thought, or perhaps still think, that whatever is non-Cantonese is "northern." Every tyro of Chinese cuisine must experience compass shock when faced with the revelation that China has more than two culinary directions!

Westerners are equally confused about the prevailing climatic conditions of certain places in China. For example, the city of Canton is at the same latitude as the southern tip of Baja California. Shanghai, on the latitude of Savannah, Georgia, can have rather cold and uncomfortable winters. Peking, often thought to be far north, is actually on the fortieth parallel—the same as Philadelphia. Its climate, however, is typical of the North China Plain, on whose rim it is situated; it can be quite hot in summer and very cold in winter, with frequent dust storms. The southern and northern boundaries of Hunan, a central province, coincide with the latitudes of Key West and St. Augustine, respectively. The borders of Szechwan province would extend from Palm Beach to Atlanta, while the northern boundary of Yünnan province is at the same latitude as Daytona Beach.

While the differences in character of the various schools of Chinese cooking are broadly geographical, they are not well described by the simple designations often used—northern, southern, Shanghai, and the like. The list that follows is organized according to cities, provinces, and groups of provinces. It starts with Hopei province in the northeast, below Inner Mongolia, and roughly follows a course down the eastern seaboard and across the southern coast. (See the map on page 3.) It proceeds through the central, southwestern, and western provinces, and finally to the northwest. Although an effort has been made to touch upon all sections of China, many individual provinces have not been mentioned since their regional fare does not substantially contribute to China's culinary profile.

1. The *Honan, Hopei,* and *Shantung* schools of cooking are frequently grouped together. The provinces that give these schools their names are located in the eastern and northeastern parts of China. Dishes of these areas are generally delicate and less oily than those of most other regions, particularly the western provinces.

Another type of cooking associated with these provinces is so-called country cooking, which uses garlic and scallions in fair abundance. Examples of such country dishes are *Moo Shu Pork* (see Szechwan Menu: Pork, No. 1), and Sweet and Sour Fish (see Szechwan Menu: Seafood, No. 1), a Honan specialty. (For a Cantonese variation of Sweet and Sour Fish, see Cantonese Menu: Seafood, No. 27.)

2. *Peking,* in Hopei province, is considered by many to be the center of a quite distinct type of cooking. Actually, its cuisine derives from four backgrounds: (*a*) the local cooking of Shantung and Hopei, (*b*) Chinese Moslem cooking of Inner Mongolia and Sinkiang, which features roasting and barbecuing of lamb and beef, (*c*) imperial kitchen fare, exemplified by the sweet-sour dishes of Honan, and (*d*) the cooking of the lower Yangtze region (Hupei and Anhwei provinces), Fukien, Kwangtung, and Szechwan. Although all these styles are represented in the Peking School, Hopei, Shantung, and Moslem dishes predominate. A typically Peking method of cooking is *chiang pao,* which means "to sizzle with brown bean paste." (See Szechwan Menu: Chicken, No. 6; Pork, No. 8; and Beef, No. 7.)

3. *Kiangsu* and *Chekiang* provinces, on the eastern coast south of

Shantung, are best known for their *hung shao* dishes (see, in Chapter 2, Cooking Methods: No. 15, red-cooking). General cuisine of the locale includes seafood, meats, and vegetables.

Shanghai (in Kiangsu) is often considered the culinary center of these eastern provinces. Practically all local regional dishes can be found here, including *Lion's Head*, from Yangchow, a famous specialty of the area (see Szechwan Menu: Pork, No. 11).

4. *Fukien* province, also on the eastern coast, south of Chekiang, specializes in wonderful fish dishes and clear soups. Except for paperwrapped foods, such as chicken and shrimp, which have their origins in this province, Fukienese cuisine is not well known outside China.

5. *Kwangtung* of which Canton is the capital, is the southernmost province of China. Situated in the southeast along the South China Sea, it has the longest coastline of any province. Besides the excellence of its many seafood dishes, Kwangtung is known for an array of preparations that covers the entire taste spectrum. Its essentially tropical climate and abundant rainfall make it an exceedingly fertile area where fruits, vegetables, and rice flourish. The Cantonese school is considered by many gourmets to be the finest of all the Chinese schools of cooking. Although one might be hard put to judge its supremacy, it is at least obvious that Kwangtung province has the most varied cuisine of any. A large variety of native produce and a traditional dedication to the preparation of food result in a cuisine of tremendous scope. Though such diversity makes it difficult to single out specialties, some general observations can be made: (*a*) dishes of this area are often served with more sauce than dishes of locales farther north or west; (*b*) sauces are thickened more frequently than sauces of other regional dishes, through the use of an agent such as cornstarch; (*c*) preparations are generally oilier than those served along the coast to the north, but not so oily as those of the western areas; and (*d*) more vegetables than meat are customarily used.

6. *Szechwan, Hunan, Kweichow,* and *Yünnan* are usually referred to as the western provinces, even though Hunan is centrally situated. Cuisines of Szechwan, Hunan, and Kweichow are similar enough to each other to be grouped together, especially outside China. For many years the mountainous terrain of these inland provinces prohibited the importation of salt, so spices and hot peppers were used instead. The absence of salt-water fish in these parts is compensated for by the use of a marinade that suggests that rare and coveted delicacy. Such "fish-

flavored" dishes are translated on English-language menus as "garlic sauce" preparations. Fresh-water and river fish, particularly carp, are used for such dishes as Dry-Cooked Carp (see Szechwan Menu: Seafood, No. 3).

Since rather good growing conditions prevail in this area, many kinds of vegetables are cultivated. Generally speaking, the cuisine is (a) hot, spicy, and oily; (b) makes little use of thickening agents; and (c) has more meat than other regional cuisines. Hunanese cooking is known to use even greater quantities of cayenne and chili pepper than Szechwan. Kweichow cooking, while having features common to this locale, is not familiar outside of China. Yünnan, a third of whose population is comprised of non-Chinese ethnic groups, such as the Chingpo, Thai, Tibetan, and Yi peoples, is not known for any particular school of cooking, although it does have a few specialties.

7. *Tsinghai* and *Kansu* provinces in northwest China are agriculturally poor, and not typified by any great schools of cooking. The sparse grasslands of Tsinghai are used for cattle grazing, and only about 7 percent of Kansu is cultivated. Long and severe winters in both provinces make it impossible to grow anything but millet, corn, and wheat.

The above list purposely omits any reference to "Mandarin" cuisine, a term frequently used by Westerners to mean northern cooking. The word "mandarin," which is not of Chinese origin, is the generic term used by English-speaking people for Chinese officials of the old regime. While it is a fact that certain restaurants call themselves "Mandarin," they aspire to an eclectic menu, borrowing from many regions. The underlying idea may be an identification with the more cosmopolitan tastes of the well-traveled mandarins of old China. To confound the issue even more, the word "Mandarin" is also used for the standard dialect of China; thus many non-Chinese make the understandable error of assuming that if Cantonese-speaking people prepared Cantonese-style food, then Mandarin-speaking people must prepare Mandarin-style food.

Given the complexity of its origins, Chinese cooking in America can readily be imagined as a rich tapestry woven over a long period of time. Chinese of many provinces now reside in America, and the culinary traditions they brought with them will continue to expand our appreciation of their food. But while our general understanding of the Chinese kitchen has increased, Chinese cuisine in America remains largely an undiscovered feast. This guide, which details many facets of the cuisine of China, will perhaps aid in its discovery.

2

MANNERS ANd MORES:
SOME pRELIMINARIES TO diNING

Anyone seriously interested in Chinese food should know how to use Chinese tableware and what to do with various table condiments. It is also helpful when ordering to know something of the various methods of preparing Chinese dishes. Knowledge of these things affords the diner a degree of confidence and adds immensely to dining pleasure; and the curiosities of Chinese cuisine and its manners are interesting in themselves.

When queried about rules of etiquette for dining Chinese-style, many Chinese will skirt the issue and assert that the most important considerations are appreciation and enjoyment of the food. However direct and comforting this may sound, it is not entirely true, since all cultures abide to some degree by rather specific patterns of dining behavior, and will judge outsiders on the basis of their manners. The restaurant-goer who seeks entry into the inner sanctum of Chinese culinary pleasures must observe the basics of Chinese etiquette. Though not as complex as those of some other cultures, Chinese table manners may pose some problems for the Westerner. A few sources of perplexity are clarified below.

CHOPSTICKS

Though it is not absolutely necessary to eat with chopsticks in a Chinese restaurant, if you want to be accepted as a serious student of Chinese cuisine, especially in a Cantonese restaurant, the use of chopsticks is essential. The Cantonese subculture in America is largely a closed one, and Cantonese waiters tend to be circumspect with Westerners who order Chinese food and then proceed to eat it with a fork. Though eating Chinese-style may make you feel clumsy at first, it is a small price to pay for the rewards you will reap.

I strongly recommend an empirical approach to chopsticks: Use them first and *then* figure out how they work. While still a fledgling struggling unsuccessfully with this mode of eating, I received so much advice on finger position that the entire subject became anathema. Fortunately, I remembered a friend who taught me to ride a bicycle by jumping on his own bike, riding off, and shouting back, "This is the way to do it!" To avoid embarrassment analogous to that of falling off the bicycle, I took home a set of chopsticks and compelled myself to eat with them. The method worked well and rather quickly.

Chopsticks are eating utensils, and whether you are a neophyte in their use or have already acquired agility with them, it is *definitely* a breach of etiquette to toy with them. Don't impale morsels with one stick or use both sticks in the manner of knitting needles. Many people who really should know better must think themselves invisible when dining in Chinese restaurants, so engaged are they in a variety of childish chopstick activities. A certain Englishwoman of my acquaintance exhibits the refined manners of her heritage when on her own turf, but in a Chinese restaurant her antics with chopsticks range from unseemliness to downright vulgarity.

SOUP

Though soup is served at the beginning of a meal, Chinese do not consider it merely as a first course. After each person at the table has been served one or two bowlfuls, the remainder is used as a beverage throughout the meal. Most non-Chinese empty the tureen before the other dishes arrive, but if you wish to dine *de rigueur*, put some of the soup aside and ask the waiter to leave the soup bowls and tureen on the table. The bowls may then be filled with more soup when desired. If the soup contains many vegetables, it is regarded as a dish to be enjoyed along with the rest of the meal.

MAIN COURSES

Main dishes—that is, the courses that follow soup—are placed upon the table just as soon as the chef has prepared them. In Cantonese cuisine, if shellfish such as crab or clams has been ordered, it is usually brought out first, since it is intended as a kind of small or appetizer course. When a whole fish is one of the selections, it is usually brought a bit later. The first portion of the fish should be served by one person to all others at the table. Later the guests may help themselves. All dishes should be eaten more or less simultaneously; that is, you should take a bit from one dish, then some from another. When a sweet and sour dish is chosen, it is wise to have a variety of other flavors as well, and not to eat too much of the sweet and sour dish at one time, since sweet flavors tend to mute the appetite. Although authentically Chinese, sweet and sour dishes are not eaten nearly as frequently by the Chinese themselves as by Westerners.

It seems to be a general practice of Chinese restaurants to bring covered serving dishes to the tables of Western diners, and uncovered ones to the tables of Chinese patrons. This practice is probably due to the Western predilection for hot food; but whatever the reason, if covered dishes are brought to your table, ask the waiter to remove the covers and take them away. Otherwise the food will overcook in the confined heat, and will no longer be authentically Chinese.

RICE AND RICE BOWLS

A basic tenet in the philosophy of Chinese cuisine is that rice is the most important part of a meal, and all other dishes accompaniments. Indeed, the word for cooked rice in the Chinese language *means* food. The usual way of eating rice is directly from the individual rice bowl. If these bowls seem too large to hold with one hand, or if the contents are shared with others at the same table, spoon some of the rice into the smaller soup bowl that you have judiciously retained, and which will also be used for more soup whenever it is empty of rice. The other food is then picked up with chopsticks and eaten together with the rice or spooned in small quantities atop the rice. Many Chinese prefer to place bits from all the dishes onto a plate and then transfer the food from there to the rice in its bowl. Eating from a flat dish with chopsticks is not only anomalous but very difficult when you reach the last few grains of rice. On the other hand, if your chopstick skill is still wanting, serve yourself some rice on a plate and place small quantities of each dish (without mixing them) on or around the rice and use a fork. Whichever method you choose, don't inundate the rice with sauce early in the meal. It is quite proper to enjoy the sauces, but save them for the end. In fact, the Chinese usually eat most of their rice toward the end of the meal.

It has been my observation that Cantonese restaurants generally serve more rice than other Chinese restaurants. Whether this is a true regional difference or just a peculiarity of the restaurants I have visited, I cannot say. Although you may order more rice, some establishments may charge for additional bowls.

SOY SAUCE AND OTHER CONDIMENTS

Chinese rarely, if ever, use soy sauce, salt, or pepper at the table. Since these are considered seasonings for use in the *preparation* of food, their use at the table is an unfavorable reflection on the chef's proficiency. While it is a fact that most Chinese restaurants do display bottles of soy sauce on the table, it is a dark, thick variety used only for cooking and not as a table condiment. Occasionally bottles of pale, thin soy sauce called "light soy" are found on the tables of some restaurants. Although this too is a cooking soy, its use at the table has gained some grudging acceptance among Chinese.

Szechwan-style restaurants ordinarily have bottles of white vinegar as well as light soy sauce on the table. The vinegar is commonly used with dumplings (see Szechwan Menu: Appetizers, Nos. 4–6), either by itself or combined with soy sauce. Red-hot oil is another condiment enjoyed with these dumplings. Dilute this fiery concoction with soy sauce when you first try it.

Many dishes are customarily eaten with certain dips, sauces, or flavored salts placed in small individual saucers beside each service or in slightly larger vessels in the center of the table. If you are puzzled over what to dip in what sauce, the waiter will be happy to tell you. The dishes of mustard and sweet-sour sauce that frequently accompany Chinese fare are almost never used by the Chinese themselves when dining. Although it is not a serious breach of table etiquette to use them, it does seem to be yet another case of the imposition of American taste preferences on Chinese cuisine.

TEA AND OTHER BEVERAGES

Contrary to what most people seem to think, tea is not drunk throughout a Chinese meal. As mentioned above, soup functions as a mealtime beverage; tea is drunk near or at the end of the meal. Oolong and jasmine teas are the ones most frequently used, and they are never taken with sugar or milk by the Chinese. Coffee is not available in an authentic Chinese restaurant, even though it is the usual beverage served in pastry shops.

Wine and beer are popular accompaniments of Chinese food among both Chinese and non-Chinese. If you enjoy wine with your meal, a dry white variety is a good choice. Although some Chinese wines are available, they do not seem to be drunk often at mealtime.

When water is served in a Chinese restaurant, avoid the temptation to swallow it by the gallon. This is a fairly common practice among Westerners and it can produce a most uncomfortable bloated feeling. It is better to quench your thirst with a bit of soup and then later with tea. If you are really thirsty, then do take some water, of course, but under no circumstances should you drink soda pop with the food.

DESSERT

Quite early in the development of Chinese cuisine, the concept of the "five flavors" was already known. A philosophic idea, meant to achieve complement and contrast in food, these five flavors were described in a fourth-century B.C. Taoist treatise as *bitter, salt, sour, hot,* and *sweet*. According to the Chinese esthetic, the best-planned menu is one that incorporates all or as many as possible of the five flavors into one meal. All the same, the Chinese do not generally include sweet flavors as part of the ordinary mealtime fare, and certainly do not share the Western custom of eating dessert at the end of a meal. Although the Chinese have many kinds of sweet pastries, tarts, puddings, honeyed fruits, and the like, these are consumed at teatime or with coffee—quite apart from the regular meal. Most Chinese restaurants, however, have made concessions to Western taste in the form of ice cream, almond cookies, and the delightful if nonauthentic fortune cookies.

FOOD-PIECE SIZES AND COOKING METHODS

The size into which food is cut before cooking is an important element in Chinese cuisine and figures prominently on the Chinese menu—for example, "snow peas with chicken *slices*" and "roast pork, *diced.*" Cooking methods are also included in the names of certain dishes (Deep-Fried Chicken Wings); this does not seem unusual to Westerners, who are familiar with "home-fried potatoes" and "poached eggs." Brief descriptions of food-piece sizes and cooking methods follow.

————Sizes of Food Pieces————

Pronunciation Key: Cantonese/Mandarin*
Chinese cooking technique requires the cutting or slicing of ingredients into specific sizes for particular dishes. Morever, *all* the ingredients of a dish are generally cut accordingly. For example, if a recipe calls for diced pork, the accompanying ingredients will be diced also, or at least cut in an equivalent size. Thus, the morsel size of a recipe's main ingredient indicates more or less the piece size of its other ingredients as well.

1. WHOLE PIECES 仁 yan/jen
   Used for whole shrimp or whole almonds.

2. SLICED 片 pin/p'ien
   As in sliced pork, chicken, or shrimp.

* Phonetics for the Chinese characters are shown in both Cantonese and Mandarin throughout the book. When only one of these is shown, that particular method or expression is used only by that language-speaking group. For example, *Kung Pao* (Cooking Methods No. 18) is a style of food preparation found primarily in Szechwan restaurants, where Mandarin is usually the accepted language of the owners and waiters. The purpose of these phonetics is not to encourage the reader to speak Chinese, but rather to provide some idea of how the characters are pronounced. A pronunciation guide is given in the Appendix.

3. SMALL PIECES 碌 luk/lu

Used specifically for pieces of chicken that have not been boned and for shrimp cooked in the shell.

4. CHUNKS 球 kao/ch'iu

Used for shelled or breaded shrimp and for pieces of deboned chicken.

5. DICED 丁 ding/ting

Half-inch cubes of pork, shrimp, or chicken.

6. FINELY DICED 粒 lap/li

$\frac{1}{16}$–$\frac{1}{8}$-inch cubes, usually of pork or chicken.

7. SHREDDED 絲 see/ssu

Very fine strips of pork or chicken.

8. CHOPPED OR MINCED 鬆 soong/sung

Finely chopped, as for minced squab or chopped pork.

9. FINELY MINCED 蓉 yung/jung

Almost puréed, such as the chicken in Bird's Nest Soup. Actually this character does not appear on the menu itself. For artistic or poetic purposes the homonym 茸 or 蓉 is used instead. Interestingly, since all three characters have the same sound as the Chinese word for velvet, the dishes that are prepared with such finely minced chicken are called "chicken velvet" in English.

———Cooking Methods———

Pronunciation Key: Cantonese/Mandarin

Some of the cooking methods described below are rather specialized, in that they are peculiar to a particular region. All of them, however, are used in the preparation of dishes included in this guide.

The translations of the names of Chinese cooking methods on English menus are very often inaccurate. For example, a red-cooked dish (No. 15) may be rendered in English as something with brown sauce, and a dry-cooked dish (No. 16) may be translated as a dish made with hot, spicy sauce. Another kind of ambivalence is noted in the single character 炒, found in No. 2 and No. 3, to represent two quite dissimilar methods of cooking, stir-frying and sautéeing. The Chinese chef can tell from the context of a recipe, or on the basis of his experience, which is meant; but the English translation makes indiscriminate use of the term "sautéed."

1. HEATING OR BOILING 煮 jü/chu

> Although this character ordinarily means boiling, it is also used to indicate pan-frying. (Cantonese Menu: Seafood, Nos. 22, 28, 29.)

2. STIR-FRYING 炒 chau/ch'ao

> The ingredients are cooked in a small amount of oil and stirred constantly. (Szechwan Menu: Vegetables, No. 4.)

3. SAUTÉEING OR BRAISING 炒 chau/ch'ao

> Although the character is the same as that used for stir-frying, in this method the ingredients are coated with hot grease and then cooked in their own juices in a covered pan. (Cantonese Menu: Seafood, No. 20.)

4. OIL-SPLASHING OR SHOWER-FRYING 油淋 yau lin/yu lin

> Fowl prepared this way is first parboiled, then splashed with hot oil. Shower-fried fish is held in a vertical position while the hot oil is splashed over it. (Szechwan Menu: Fowl, No. 20.)

5. DEEP-FAT FRYING 炸 jau/cha

> Deep-fat frying is used for shrimp, fish, or fowl, which may be plain or batter-dipped. (Cantonese Menu: Fowl, No. 1.)

6. DOUBLE-FRYING (not to be confused with double-sautéeing)
> This method really has no name in Chinese. It is simply a combination of oil-splashing followed by deep-frying. (Szechwan Menu: Fowl, No. 1.)

7. DOUBLE-SAUTÉEING 回鍋 hui kuo (Mandarin only)
> This method, whose characters literally mean "return to the pot," is the one used for the well-known Twice-Cooked Pork. The meat is first simmered whole, then sliced and sautéed. (Szechwan Menu: Pork, No. 4.)

8. FRICASEEING 炆 mun (Cantonese only)
> Ingredients are first browned, then simmered in sauce until cooked. (Cantonese Menu: Seafood, No. 54.)

9. CLEAR-COOKING 清 ching/ch'ing
> The food is slowly cooked in water containing very little or no seasoning, and the broth is then served as a soup. (Cantonese Menu: Soups, No. 7.) "Clear-cooking" also includes clear-steaming and clear-simmering, in which the flavoring agents are, again, either absent or minimal.

10. STEAMING 蒸 ting/cheng
> The food is cooked on a rack placed above boiling water in a closed container. (Cantonese Menu: Beef, No. 5.)

11. DOUBLE-BOILER SIMMERING 燉 dun (Cantonese only)
> This method is similar to ordinary double-boiler cooking, except that the upper vessel, in which the food is placed, contains stock. Therefore, as the ingredients are being heated by the boiling water in the lower vessel, they are also simmering in the stock. (Cantonese Menu: Soups, No. 16.)

12. WHITE-WATER COOKING 白水 bak sui (Cantonese only)
> The term "white water" means not only that the cooking water has nothing added to it, but that it is not boil-

ing when the food is placed in it. For example, fish cooked in this manner requires the water to be first brought to the boil and then removed from the heat. The whole fish is then lowered into the water and allowed to poach. Flavorings and garnishes are added afterward. (Cantonese Menu: Seafood, No. 24.)

13. STEWING 扒 pa (Cantonese only)

Generally this term indicates food that is braised or stewed for a long time, during which it becomes thoroughly coated with its own gravy. Our Swiss steak is a fair comparison. (Cantonese Menu: Beef, No. 24.)

14. ROASTING, BARBECUING, OR GRILLING 燒 shu/shao

Meat, which is very often marinated first, is roasted in an oven or on a rack over direct heat. (Cantonese Menu: Pork, Nos. 14–18.)

15. RED-COOKING 紅燒 hung shu/hung shao

The ingredients are stewed slowly in a sauce that is largely soy. Much of the liquid boils away, leaving the food a reddish-brown color. (Cantonese Menu: Seafood, No. 4; Szechwan Menu: Seafood, No. 2.)

16. DRY-COOKING 乾 or 干 gan/kan

Used frequently in Szechwan cuisine, and sometimes called "fry-cooking," this method employs seasonings but little or no liquid. Since these dishes are cooked until almost dry, the flavors become concentrated. (Szechwan Menu: Seafood, No. 9.)

17. CHIANG PAO 醬爆 chiang pao (Mandarin only)

Literally meaning "to sizzle in bean paste," this is typically a Peking method. Lightly batter-dipped meat or poultry is first deep-fried, then combined with bean paste that has been fried and stirred with oil, sherry, and seasonings until the moisture evaporates. (Szechwan Menu: Pork, No. 8.)

18. KUNG PAO 宫保 kung pao (Mandarin only)

Kung pao literally means "palace protector," a title of rank among ancient Chinese officials. Since the family cooking of members of that rank was highly esteemed, *kung pao* came to be synonymous with fine cuisine. Although *kung pao* dishes do not comprise a particular group, since they are all different, they have come to be known in Szechwan cuisine as foods that have been prepared in a special way: Red chili peppers, usually whole, are first charred in oil and then sautéed with the other ingredients of the dish. The charring of the peppers imparts a depth to the flavor. (Szechwan Menu: Beef, No. 11.)

3

THE CANTONESE MENU

Almost all of the 350 dishes found on the Cantonese menu, other than seasonal dishes, are available at any time without advance notice. This guide lists 235. Noodle dishes, which the Chinese eat for lunch, and some dishes that are considered to be banquet fare make up the remainder.

The full Cantonese menu will not, of course, be found in specialty places such as noodle houses or dumpling shops, and certainly not in the typical neighborhood Chinese-American restaurant. Even in these neighborhood restaurants, however, with the use of this guide, one can obtain food which is much superior to that ordinarily served in such places, and certainly more interesting. While there are rather close similarities among Cantonese menus, no two restaurants will prepare the same dish in identical ways. Indeed, many restaurants employ seven or eight chefs, each of whom may add his own distinctive touch to a dish. It should also be noted that not all the dishes listed here will be available in every restaurant.

Although always important in Chinese cooking, the size of food pieces (diced, chunks) is given particular emphasis in Cantonese dishes. This is apparent in the format of the Cantonese Chinese-language menu, where dishes are often grouped according to piece size. Two chicken dishes, for example, may have essentially the same ingredients, but if one dish has chunks of chicken and the other sliced chicken, they are listed as two separate preparations. Thus one can find bitter melon with chicken chunks next to *choy sum* with chicken chunks. A bit farther on one finds bitter melon again, but this time with chicken slices, and next to this, *choy sum* with chicken slices. While this arrangement may strike the Westerner as redundant, the two bitter melon and chicken dishes *are* different from each other. The distinction is a textural one, somewhat analogous to the difference between pot roast and beef stew.

The names of dishes, as they appear in English here, may seem inverted to the Westerner—for example, Green Beans with Roast Pork rather than Roast Pork and Green Beans, or Curry with Beef instead of the more familiar Beef Curry. The reason is that both in the Chinese language and in Chinese cuisine the vegetable or flavoring is considered to be a modifier of the meat—rather like saying "vegetabled meat." In other words, when meat is prepared with a vegetable, the dish is always described in Chinese with the English equivalent of "vegetable with meat," as though the meat were a secondary ingredient.

To translate a Cantonese menu, a staggering measure of poesy, fantasy, fact, and legend has to be winnowed, sifted, and sorted. There are few Cantonese-English dictionaries, and none explain or elucidate the many flights of fancy that motivate Cantonese-speaking people in naming their dishes. As a translator I have had to rely on many scholarly sources in reaching reasoned judgments about names and origins of many dishes. When the etymology or history of a particular dish is less than certain, I have said so.

The phonetics shown next to the characters are intended only as general indications of the actual sounds. No universally accepted system of Cantonese phonetics is presently available, and so the best features of several systems for this difficult and diverse eight-tone dialect have been combined. A pronunciation guide is given in the Appendix, but untrained readers are advised not to attempt to order in Chinese. Point to the characters that show the names of your choices, and there will be a minimum of confusion.

SOUP

湯

tang

1. CHICKEN VELVET AND SHARK'S FIN SOUP

Shark's fin, first simmered in chicken broth with leeks and ginger, then seasoned with wine and sesame oil, is combined with a mixture of beaten egg white and chicken that has been ground or minced to a smooth paste (see Chapter 2: Size of Food Pieces, No. 9). Corn flour is added to the soup after it is cooked. Shredded ham and bamboo shoots are usual garnishes. An expensive dish, shark's fin soup is often served at special dinners.

gai

yung

saang

jih

鷄茸生翅

2. CHICKEN VELVET AND BIRD'S NEST SOUP

This famous banquet delicacy is indeed made with the nests of small birds, called swiftlets. The nests are simmered in chicken broth, then combined with ground or shredded chicken that has been mixed with beaten egg white, and garnished with ham and snow peas. This soup is usually thickened with cornstarch. Since birds' nests are costly, this soup is quite expensive.

gai

yung

yin

wo

鷄茸燕窩

3. SLICED CHICKEN WITH SHARK'S FIN SOUP

Shark's fin is simmered in chicken broth with leek and ginger root, seasoned with sesame oil, then garnished with sliced chicken breast and ham, and egg-flowered (as in egg-drop soup) before serving. The first two characters mean "overcooked chicken," indicating that to prepare the broth, a whole chicken is cooked until it falls off the bones. Like all shark's fin dishes, this is expensive.

lan

gai

saang

jih

爛鷄生翅

4. BEAN CURD SOUP

Clear chicken broth is the base for this delicate soup. Bamboo shoots, snow peas, sliced pork, black mushrooms, and large cubes of bean curd float in broth that is subtly flavored with either ginger root or sesame oil.

dou

fu

tang

豆腐湯

5. CHICKEN VELVET AND SWEET CORN SOUP

A mixture of puréed chicken and egg white is added to chicken broth in which fresh corn kernels have been cooked. Shredded ham and snow peas often serve as garnishes. A simplified but very good version of this lovely soup is frequently found in Cantonese restaurants, particularly in winter, when fresh corn is not available. Chicken broth is combined with cream-style corn, and thickened with cornstarch; then snow peas and freshly shredded chicken and ham are added. This soup is usually egg-flowered (as in egg-drop soup) before it is served.

gai
yung
syut
maï
tang

鷄茸粟米湯

6. CLEAR BROTH WITH SEASONAL VEGETABLE

The vegetable (usually lettuce) and a few snow peas are added to plain chicken broth that is lightly seasoned with sesame oil. A pleasant soup for warm weather.

ching
tang
sih
choy
tang

清湯時菜湯

7. CLEAR BROTH WITH FISH DUMPLING

This delicious four-season soup seems to be enjoyed by everyone. "Fish dumpling" is my own translation for what is really the swim bladder of the conger eel (see Food Notes: Swim Bladder). The swim bladder has little or no flavor of its own, and certainly no fishy taste. Here it is fried and added to chicken broth, where it assumes the texture of a light, airy dumpling and absorbs the wonderful flavors of the other ingredients. Sliced Chinese ham, snow peas, and a dash of sesame oil are added before serving.

ching
tang
yü
tou
tang

清湯魚肚湯

8. SEAWEED SOUP

For a delightful warm-weather soup, seaweed shreds, usually a type called laver, and chopped chicken or pork are simmered in clear chicken broth that is lightly flavored with sesame oil and egg-flowered (as in egg-drop soup) before serving.

ji
choy
tang

紫菜湯

9. HAM AND MUSTARD GREEN SOUP

Fresh mustard green has a slightly bitter flavor that complements the salty, smoked Smithfield ham. The clear broth usually has a bit of sliced ginger root in it. An excellent soup for any season.

fo
tuy
gai
choy
tang

火腿芥菜湯

10. BLACK MUSHROOM AND ABALONE SOUP

Slices of abalone, bamboo shoots, snow peas, and lots of wonderful black Chinese mushrooms are gently simmered in a finely flavored clear broth. Very nice for summer.

bak
gu
bau
yü
tang

北菇鮑魚湯

11. WATERCRESS SOUP

Abundant amounts of this lovely green, whose Chinese characters mean "vegetable of the Occident," are simmered in clear chicken broth flavored with ginger root. An egg is usually poached in the soup before the tureen is brought to table and the person who serves the soup portions some of the egg into each bowl with the cress and the broth. The greenery is so abundant in this soup that many people eat just a moderate quantity with the broth and reserve the remaining portion as a vegetable dish.

sai
tang
choy
yang

西洋菜湯

12. HAIR MELON SOUP

This crisp-tasting summer vegetable is called "hair melon" because of the little bristles covering its skin. It is simmered in chicken broth that is usually flavored with a bit of ginger root. Water chestnuts are sometimes added. Some Chinese menus use the characters 毛瓜 (mo gwa) for this melon.

jit
gwa
tang

節瓜湯

13. FISH SLICES AND LETTUCE IN CLEAR BROTH

Sea bass is most frequently used for this soup, but other seasonal fish can be just as good. Ginger root and soy flavor the broth. Except in France, lettuce as a cooked green is not well known in Western cuisines; but after you taste this soup, you might be inspired to experiment a bit at home.

yü

pin

saang

choy

tang

魚片生菜湯

14. PICKLED MUSTARD GREEN AND BEAN CURD SOUP

Pickled mustard green is often referred to as Chinese sauerkraut, but, though it is tart and salty like ordinary sauerkraut, it is also slightly sweet. Seasoned with ginger root and served with ham and pork slices, pickled mustard green soup makes a wonderful, full-bodied dish that is quite filling by itself.

ham

choy

dou

fu

tang

咸菜豆腐湯

15. TOMATO EGG-FLOWER SOUP

An interesting variation of the familiar egg-drop soup, this one adds the fresh and appealing flavor of tomatoes to the basic chicken broth.

fan

keh

dan

fa

tang

番茄蛋花湯

16. CLEAR-SIMMERED MUSHROOMS

Chinese mushrooms are slowly simmered in clear chicken broth and lightly flavored with sesame oil. Snow peas and bamboo shoots are sometimes added. Because of the generous quantity and high cost of the large black mushrooms, this soup is fairly expensive.

ching

dun

bak

gu

tang

清燉北菇湯

17. SEA CUCUMBER (*Bêche-de-Mer*) **AND ABALONE SOUP**
A soup for sophisticated palates, this is a clear chicken
broth in which slices of abalone and sea cucumber (a
member of the starfish family) have been simmered.
Most Westerners require time to develop a taste for
sea cucumber, since they usually find its iodine flavor
and soft, slippery texture rather strange at first.

hoi

sum

bau

yü

tang

海參鮑魚湯

18. GREEN PEA AND DICED CHICKEN SOUP
Although not an unusual soup, its flavor is delicate and
suitable for any season. The broth is egg-flowered (as
in egg-drop soup) before it is served.

ching

dou

gai

lap

tang

青豆鷄粒湯

19. WINTER MELON CUP
This fabulous soup (not to be confused with Ham and
Winter Melon Soup, often found on Szechwan
menus), is available only upon advance request—at
least one day's notice. A mélange of duck, pork,
chicken, ham, mushrooms, bamboo shoots, and gingko
nuts is simmered slowly right in the melon (hence the
term "melon cup"). When the soup is served, the
melon is scooped out along with its treasures. It is
truly banquet fare.

dung

gwa

jong

冬瓜盅

20. SLICED FRESH PORK AND MUSTARD GREEN SOUP
Pork and fresh mustard green are simmered with sliced
ginger root in chicken broth; snow peas are often added
at the end preparation. Although remarkably fresh-
tasting, this soup still has a full and hearty flavor.

yuk

pin

gai

choy

tang

肉片芥菜湯

21. RIDGED MELON SOUP WITH STRAW MUSHROOMS AND BEAN CURD

This marvelous soup, available only in summer, is almost a meal in itself. Large pieces of ridged melon (no counterpart in Western cuisines) are simmered with straw mushrooms and bean curd in a clear chicken broth.

cho gu sing gwa dou fu tang

草菇勝瓜豆腐湯

22. SOUR AND HOT SOUP

Strictly speaking, this is not a Cantonese dish, but it is usually available in Cantonese restaurants with slight variations from the familiar Szechwan version. Bamboo shoots and sliced pork are simmered with ginger root in clear broth. Light vinegar and a generous quantity of black pepper are the "sour" and "hot" ingredients, respectively. Cakes of bean curd are often added to the soup, which is egg-flowered (as in egg-drop soup) before it is served.

sün la tang

酸辣湯

23. BOTTLE GOURD MELON SOUP

The bottle gourd is a smooth-skinned, pear-shaped melon which, when cooked, is similar in texture and flavor to winter melon. Pork slices and a little ginger root are simmered in clear chicken broth with the melon pieces. Available only in summer.

pu lu gwa tang

葫蘆瓜湯

SQUAB, CHICKEN, DUCK DISHES

白 鴿　鷄　鴨 類
bak　kap　　gai　　opp　luy

1. CRISP FRIED SQUAB

Whole squab is rubbed with pepper, soy sauce, honey, and five-spice essence, then deep-fried. It is cut up into manageable portions, head included, and served with lemon wedges and savory salt, which is a mixture of Szechwan pepper (花 椒 , *hua chiao*), salt, and star anise. The lemon is squeezed over the squab pieces, which are then dipped into the savory salt and eaten with chopsticks and fingers. Fried squab makes a nice introductory nibbling course.

jau 炸
bak 白
kap 鴿

2. SOY SAUCE SQUAB

Whole squab is first sautéed in oil, then simmered in oyster sauce, soy sauce, ginger, and wine. Prepared in this way it is similar to *Soy Sauce Chicken* (see No. 30 below), but has a deeper flavor.

see 豉
yau 油
bak 白
kap 鴿

3. LEMON SQUAB

Whole squab, coated with soy sauce, is deep-fried, braised with lemon slices and ginger root, then cut up and served with lemon wedges and fresh coriander. If you have never had squab, this is an excellent introduction.

leng 檸
jap 汁
bak 白
kap 鴿

4. OYSTER SAUCE WITH SQUAB

Whole squab is deep-fried until brown, then braised with oyster sauce, scallions, and perhaps a bit of five-spice essence. It is cut up before being served and is thus easily eaten with chopsticks and fingers.

ho 蠔
yau 油
bak 白
kap 鴿

5. CHINESE MUSHROOMS AND SQUAB

After being deep-fried, the squab is cut up and lightly stewed with mushrooms and oyster sauce. Snow peas, which are usually added, give a touch of freshness.

bak
gu
wat
kap

北菇熼鴿

6. SAUTÉED SQUAB IN BITE-SIZE PIECES

Here the squab is cut up into rather small pieces (bone-in) before being sautéed with oyster sauce. Ginger root and wine may be used as additional flavors.

chau
bak
kap
luk

炒白鴿碌

7. SAUTÉED MINCED YOUNG SQUAB

Squab, pork, water chestnuts, and black mushrooms are minced together and sautéed with ginger root. Soy sauce, sesame oil, and green peas are added toward the end of preparation. This tasty mixture is wrapped in leaves of crisp romaine lettuce and eaten with fingers and chopsticks.

chau
yu
kap
soong

炒乳鴿鬆

8. YOUNG GINGER WITH SQUAB

Slices of young ginger are sautéed with small pieces of squab (bone in), then braised in a little broth. Young ginger has an almost ambrosial delicacy rather than the sharp, biting taste of mature ginger.

ji
geung
bak
luk

子羌白鴿碌

9. CRISP FRIED CHICKEN

Whole chicken is first deep-fried, then cut up and served on a bed of lettuce with lemon wedges. The delicate nutty flavor is enhanced by squeezing the lemon over the chicken. No vegetables are included.

jau
ji
gai

炸子鷄

10. FRESH FISH AND CHICKEN MORSELS

A masterful combination of sautéed chicken pieces, *bok choy*, water chestnuts, and ginger on a bed of fish filets. The filets, placed raw in the serving dish, are cooked by the heat of the chicken and vegetables. Usually available only in summer.

yü
saang
gai
kao

魚生鷄球

11. CHOY SUM (*Vegetable Heart*) WITH CHICKEN MOR-SELS

Bite-size pieces of chicken, sautéed with *choy sum*, ginger, and scallions, are served in a soy-flavored sauce that is usually thickened with corn flour. Good in any season.

choy
sum
gai
kao

菜心鷄球

12. BITTER (*Cool*) MELON WITH CHICKEN CHUNKS

Small pieces of chicken are sautéed with sliced bitter melon, scallions, ginger, black bean paste, and crushed garlic. Bitter melon has an unusual flavor and generally one must acquire a taste for it. Fresh bitter melon is available only in summer and fall; the canned vegetable, although available year-round, is inferior in flavor and texture.

leung
gwa
gai
kao

凉瓜鷄球

13. LOBSTER AND CHICKEN CHUNKS

Lobster and chicken are sautéed with snow peas, water chestnuts, and bamboo shoots, and usually flavored with oyster sauce and ginger root. This is an interesting dish because of the variety of textures.

lung
fung
gai
kao

龍鳳鷄球

14. STEAMED SALT CHICKEN

A whole chicken, aged for a few days in a heavy coating of salt, is steamed in a bit of oyster or soy sauce, cut crosswise, and served in its own juices. The simplicity of this dish does not detract from its rich, full flavor.

ting
ham
gai

蒸咸鷄

15. HAM WITH STEAMED CHICKEN

A delicate but elegant dish of finely flavored steamed chicken arranged on a platter with slices of Chinese (Smithfield) ham and garnished with fresh coriander.

fo

tuy

ting

gai

火腿蒸鶏

16. SAUSAGE STEAMED WITH CHICKEN

Chinese sausage, which is quite unlike any other, is a delicious, aromatic combination of pork, wine, sugar, salt, and soy sauce. In this dish, it is steamed with chunks of chicken, which absorb its tantalizing, spicy flavor. Chinese sausage dishes are customarily served only in fall and winter.

lap

chang

ting

gai

腊腸蒸鶏

17. BLACK BEAN SAUCE WITH CHICKEN

Small pieces of chicken (bone in) are sautéed with black bean paste, ginger, scallions, and garlic, then braised until the chicken is tender and pungent with the black bean aroma.

see

jap

gai

luk

豉汁鶏磲

18. OYSTER SAUCE WITH CHICKEN

Chicken pieces (bone in) are sautéed, then braised in oyster sauce until tender. A few snow peas are usually added to give a touch of green to the nicely browned chicken morsels.

ho

yau

gai

luk

蠔油鶏磲

19. TOMATOES WITH CHICKEN

Another simple but piquant chicken dish, in which small pieces of chicken (bone in) are braised with tomatoes, black bean sauce, garlic, ginger, and scallions. An interesting dish that uses a Western vegetable but retains its authentic Chinese character.

fan

keh

gai

luk

番茄鶏磲

20. CHINESE MUSHROOMS STEAMED WITH CHICKEN

A special treat for people like me who can't get enough of the big, meaty mushrooms, in this instance seasoned with soy and ginger root. No vegetables are included, so order at least one other dish prepared with a green vegetable.

bak
gu
ting
gai

北菇蒸鷄

21. BITTER (Cool) MELON WITH CHICKEN

Morsels of chicken (bone in) are sautéed with garlic, ginger root, scallions, black bean paste, and sliced bitter melon. Really delicious if you have acquired a taste for bitter melon.

leung
gwa
gai
luk

凉瓜鷄碌

22. WALNUTS WITH DICED CHICKEN

Chicken and fried walnuts are combined in a light sauce flavored with soy sauce, wine, and ginger root. The bland chicken flavor goes very well with the rather musty taste of the walnuts.

hop
tou
gai
ding

合桃鷄丁

23. ALMONDS WITH DICED CHICKEN

Chicken cubes are sautéed with almonds (either whole or in pieces) and scallions, then seasoned with sesame oil and wine. A familiar favorite of Westerners for decades, this dish is commonly known as Chicken Almond Ding.

hang
yan
gai
ding

杏仁鷄丁

24. GREEN PEAS WITH DICED CHICKEN

Green garden peas (not snow peas) are combined with the chicken and carrots, both diced, to make a very attractive-looking dish as well as a pleasant-tasting one.

ching
dou
gai
ding

青豆鷄丁

25. Snow Peas with Sliced Chicken

Hardly exotic, but still a very good dish, the chicken and snow peas are combined in a light gravy that is usually seasoned with ginger root and wine.

sut
dou
gai
pin

雪豆鷄片

26. Ham with Sliced Chicken

Chicken is braised with ham, *bok choy*, bamboo shoots, and water chestnuts. The ham gives a nice, salty, smoky flavor to the other ingredients. A bit of wine is sometimes added to the gravy.

fo
tuy
gai
pin

火腿鷄片

27. Bitter (*Cool*) Melon with Sliced Chicken

Chicken is sautéed with garlic, ginger root, black bean paste, and sliced bitter melon. When properly prepared (that is, not overcooked), the melon has a firm texture and a somewhat acrid flavor.

leung
gwa
gai
pin

凉瓜鷄片

28. One Chicken, Three Flavors

A whole fresh chicken is prepared as three different dishes. These usually are: (1) a soup with vegetables added, (2) small chunks sautéed with *bok choy* or *choy sum*, (3) bite-size portions prepared with sweet and sour sauce or black bean sauce. When this dish is ordered, it counts as a soup plus two dishes.

yat
gai
sam
mei

一鷄三味

29. Asparagus and Sliced Chicken

Fresh-cut asparagus is braised together with chicken in a little soy sauce and wine. The asparagus is cooked only until barely tender.

lei
sun
gai
pin

露芛鷄片

30. SOY SAUCE CHICKEN
Whole chicken is braised in a mixture of dark and
light soy sauces, sherry, tangerine peel, star anise, cinnamon bark, and a bit of sugar until the skin is dark
brown. The chicken is hacked crosswise, served at room
temperature with the sauce poured over, and garnished
with scallions and fresh coriander. The firm, meaty
morsels are delectable dipped in the aromatic sauce.

see

yau

gai

豉
油
鷄

31. FRESH GINGER ROOT WITH BRAISED CHICKEN
Pieces of fried chicken are slowly braised with an abundance of ginger root, sliced or in chunks. No vegetables are included. This is a dish for ginger addicts;
if you are not familiar with the taste of ginger root,
don't begin your acquaintance with this dish.

saang

geung

guk

gai

生
姜
焗
鷄

32. CURRY CHICKEN
Many people are not aware of Chinese curry dishes.
They are excellent, and of about medium hotness. In
this one, chunks of chicken (bone in) are sautéed in
oil with curry powder and thick slices of onion. The
liquid used is either chicken or beef broth, since Chinese curries do not use milk.

ga

lei

gai

luk

咖
哩
鷄
礫

33. YOUNG GINGER WITH SLICED CHICKEN
Slices of young ginger are sautéed with chicken, then
braised until the ginger is cooked but still crisp. A very
piquant dish, available only in summer. The ginger
makes it quite hot to the taste, so be cautious.

ji

geung

gai

pin

子
姜
鷄
片

34. LOTUS ROOT AND SLICED CHICKEN
Slices of the crisp, crunchy "root" are sautéed with
chicken, scallions, snow peas, and cloud ears (tree fungus). Lotus root is similar to fresh coconut in taste
and texture and is thoroughly delicious when prepared
in this way.

ling

au

gai

pin

蓮
藕
鷄
片

35. WHITE CUT CHICKEN

I once heard this delightful dish described as "plain
boiled chicken," which is akin to calling crêpes "flap-
jacks." A whole chicken is boiled for a short time in
water with leeks, ginger root, and wine. Then, with
the flame turned off, it is left to steep until tender,
after which it is rubbed with oil, cut crosswise, and
served warm or at room temperature. Particularly delicious when dipped in oyster sauce. This method, unlike ordinary boiling, preserves the texture of the meat.

bak

chit

gai

36. FRESH MUSHROOMS AND CHICKEN

The mushrooms usually used in this dish are the small,
pointed-hat straw mushrooms. These are lightly braised
in oyster sauce together with small pieces of chicken,
water chestnuts, bamboo shoots, and snow peas.
Note: Although the term "fresh" is used, the mushrooms are canned. On the Chinese menu the term
"fresh mushrooms" includes all mushrooms that are
not dried.

sin

gu

gai

kao

37. SATELLITE CHICKEN

Cut-up boneless Soy Sauce Chicken is arranged on a
platter and surrounded by sautéed fresh mustard
greens, which form the "satellite" of the chicken. This
is one of the elegant dishes frequently served as banquet fare.

wai

sying

gai

38. GOLDEN FLOWER JADE TREE CHICKEN

"Golden flower" is a special variety of Chinese (Smithfield) ham, and "jade tree" refers to a green vegetable,
typically Chinese broccoli or mustard green. Pieces of
steamed marinated chicken, arranged alternately with
ham slices and surrounded with the crisp vegetable,
become an artful dish worthy of its poetic name. This
is generally a rather expensive dish.

gum

wah

yut

syu

gai

39. CHICKEN LIVERS WITH SLICED CHICKEN (literally "Phoenix Livers")
Both chicken and livers are sliced, sautéed with *bok choy*, and seasoned with a bit of wine and sesame oil. Try this even if you don't like chicken livers.

fung 鳳
gan 肝
gai 鷄
pin 片

40. DEEP-FRIED CHICKEN GIBLETS
Often served as an *hors d'oeuvre*, these deep-fried chicken giblets are flavored with ginger root, star anise, soy sauce, and wine. Many known giblet-haters make an exception of this dish.

jau 炸
jum 珍
gan 肝

41. DEEP-FRIED CHICKEN WINGS
Chicken wings, first brushed with egg and cornstarch, then deep-fried, are served on a bed of lettuce with lemon wedges. Prepared in this way they make a light and crunchy first course.

jau 炸
gai 鷄
yih 翼

42. LEMON CHICKEN WINGS
Chicken wings are first deep-fried, then braised with lemon slices. The lemon-juice sauce makes this a delectably piquant dish, refreshing any time of year but particularly in summer.

leng 檸
jap 汁
gai 鷄
yih 翼

43. KETCHUP CHICKEN WINGS
Deep-fried chicken wings and a vegetable such as snow peas or *bok choy* are braised in stock, ketchup, and wine. The flavor is full-bodied and tart.

keh 茄
jap 汁
gai 鷄
yih 翼

44. OYSTER SAUCE CHICKEN WINGS

Soy sauce–coated chicken wings are first deep-fried, then braised with oyster sauce and a bit of wine. A green vegetable such as *choy sum* is sometimes included in this flavorsome dish.

ho
yau
gai
yih

蠔油鷄翼

45. GOLDEN NEEDLE CHICKEN WINGS

Chicken wings are first marinated in ginger, soy sauce and *hoisin* sauce, then braised with Chinese mushrooms and golden needles (lily buds). The golden needles add an interesting texture and fruity flavor to the sauce.

gum
jum
gai
yih

金針鷄翼

46. THREE-INGREDIENT ROAST DUCK

Although the ingredients may vary, the usual ones are shredded ham, abalone, and duck sautéed with *bok choy* and oyster sauce. This is a rather unlikely combination, but it tastes very good.

sam
see
fo
opp

三絲火鴨

47. SAUTÉED SHREDDED ROAST DUCK

Roast duck is cut in strips and sautéed with pieces of *bok choy* and oyster sauce. Ginger root is sometimes added for flavor.

chau
fo
opp
see

炒火鴨絲

48. ARHAT DUCK

This is Arhat's Feast (see Vegetables, No. 12) with shredded duck, and the flavors, like those of Arhat's Feast, are pungent and exotic.

lo
han
opp

羅漢鴨

49. OYSTER SAUCE WITH DUCK FEET

The Chinese can perform delicious wonders with even the lowliest things. Sautéed duck feet in oyster sauce is a good example. Nice to nibble on while waiting for the other dishes.

ho

yau

opp

jaang

蠔油鴨掌

50. HEART OF CHOY SUM (*Vegetable Heart*) WITH DUCK

Chunks of duck that have been deep-fried and braised in oyster sauce with ginger root, star anise, and wine are served with the vegetable and garnished with strips of Smithfield ham. Although the flavors are distinctive, they are not overpowering, and thus go well with most other dishes.

choy

dan

bat

opp

菜肥扒鴨

51. COLD PLATTER WITH ROAST DUCK

Morsels of cold roast duck are temptingly arranged on a platter with sliced ginger, carrot shreds, pickled scallions, and ham. In another variation, strips of cold roast duck are combined with green pepper, tomatoes, pickled scallions, pineapple, and lychees. A sauce of *hoisin* and ketchup is used as a garnish. Either version of this summer dish makes an excellent appetizer or "one more dish that's not too much."

leung

ban

fo

opp

涼辦火鴨

52. ROAST DUCK (*Canton-style*)

A whole duck, salted inside and out, is filled with a mixture of garlic, scallions, onions, fresh coriander, star anise, peppercorns, oil, sherry, soy sauce, and sugar. The duck is then sewn up and, while roasting, is basted with honey and wine vinegar so that the skin becomes dark, shiny, and crisp. Chinese in this country often prepare turkey in this fashion.

fo

opp

OR

shu

opp

火鴨（燒鴨）

53. CHINESE MUSHROOMS WITH DUCK

Cut-up roast duck is braised in oyster sauce with these
wonderful, big, meaty mushrooms, usually left whole.
Some dish with a green vegetable goes well with this
one.

bak

gu

bat

opp

北菇扒鴨

54. WEST LAKE DUCK

Named after the famed and beautiful West Lake in
Hang Chow, the abode of many poets and scholars,
this is a lovely concoction of duck that has first been
deep-fried, then braised with sliced ham, bamboo
shoots,' water chestnuts, black mushroom strips, and
ginger root. Star anise gives this dish an elusive, aromatic flavor.

sai

wu

opp

西湖鴨

55. SWEET AND SOUR DUCK FEET

Prepared in much the same way as Oyster Sauce with
Duck Feet. Because of the sweetness, this dish is usually eaten toward the end of the meal.

tim

sün

opp

jaang

甜酸鴨掌

BEEF DISHES

牛　肉　類
ngau　*yuk*　*luy*

1. SAUTÉED BEEF CUBES (*Steak Kew*)
Chunks of tender beef are sautéed in oyster sauce, with
snow peas sometimes added. Adapted to the preference
of Westerners by an increase in the meat portion,
Steak Kew has become a favorite dish. Chinese do not
eat large quantities of meat in any single dish. Since
there is no word for "steak" in Chinese, the second
two characters are used as phonetic approximations of
the word. Don't say "sik dik"; say "s'dik."

chau
sik
dik
kao

2. CHINESE BROCCOLI WITH BEEF
This broccoli is sharper in flavor than the American
variety. It is cut in rather large pieces and sautéed with
strips of marinated beef and ginger root, then combined
with soy or oyster sauce and sherry. This dish and No.
7 are fine examples of the stir-fry method, which
leaves the vegetables very crisp and fresh-tasting.

gai
lan
ngau
yuk

3. PICKLED MUSTARD GREEN WITH BEEF
Often called Chinese sauerkraut, pickled mustard green
has a blend of sweet-salty-sour tastes. In this dish it is
sautéed with strips of marinated beef. Pickled mustard
green is especially delicious in late summer when it is
just half-soured.

ham
choy
ngau
yuk

4. OYSTER SAUCE WITH BEEF
This familiar favorite combines oyster sauce and soy
sauce with sautéed beef, ginger root, and scallions. A
few snow peas are often added.

ho
yau
ngau
yuk

5. PRESERVED KOHLRABI (*Szechwan Cabbage*) STEAMED WITH BEEF

This crunchy vegetable gives the beef a hot, salty flavor that is faintly anise-like. A very good dish for winter, but takes some getting used to.

jya

choy

ting

ngau

yuk

搾菜蒸牛肉

6. HAM STEAMED WITH BEEF

Strips of Chinese (Smithfield) ham are steamed with beef, then garnished with sautéed snow peas and scallions. The salty ham combines well with the bland beef.

fo

tuy

ting

ngau

yuk

火腿蒸牛肉

7. CHOY SUM (*Vegetable Heart*) WITH BEEF

Strips of beef are sautéed with pieces of cabbage heart, scallions, and ginger. A bit of soy sauce may be added to accent the rather delicate flavor of the vegetable.

choy

sum

ngau

yuk

菜心牛肉

8. MUSHROOMS WITH BEEF CUBES (*Steak Kew*)

In this variation of the familiar favorite Steak Kew, tender beef chunks are braised with straw mushrooms, *bok choy*, water chestnuts, and bamboo shoots.

sin

gu

sik

dik

kao

鮮菇市的球

9. SOURED BAMBOO SHOOTS STEAMED WITH BEEF

Bamboo shoots that have been pickled in brine are
steamed with strips of beef, then combined with oyster sauce or soy sauce. The tartness of the shoots per-
meates the beef, making a flavorsome dish for any
time of year.

sun

yi

ting

ngau

yuk

莳衣蒸牛肉

10. WINTER VEGETABLE (*Preserved Celery Cabbage*) STEAMED WITH BEEF

The preserved cabbage imparts a garlicky, salty, and
fermented flavor to the beef strips. Novices are advised
to eat just a small amount at first. The rather strong
taste makes this dish more suitable for winter eating.

dung

choy

ting

ngau

yuk

冬菜蒸牛肉

11. SNOW PEAS WITH BEEF

This fresh-tasting dish, made of slices of beef sautéed
with Chinese peapods and ginger root, then seasoned
with soy sauce, is well known and liked by almost
everyone.

sut

dou

ngau

yuk

雪豆牛肉

12. YÜNNAN HAM WITH STEAMED BEEF

Beef slices are steamed with soy sauce, sherry, and ginger, then combined with strips of ham. Yünnan ham,
a specialty of this province, is yet another variety of
Chinese Smithfield-type ham.

yün

tuy

ting

ngau

yuk

雲腿蒸牛肉

13. BEAN CURD WITH BEEF
Marinated beef slices are braised in oyster sauce with cubed bean curd, ginger root, scallions, and sometimes snow peas. A good introduction to the bland, custard-like fresh bean curd. It is unfortunate that the sauce is often thickened with too much cornstarch, thereby detracting from the delicacy of the flavors.

dou
fu
ngau
yuk

豆腐牛肉

14. BITTER (*Cool*) MELON WITH BEEF
Slices of beef are sautéed with garlic, ginger, scallions, and black bean paste, then braised with sliced bitter melon. As with all the bitter melon dishes, it may have to be tried more than once before the unusual flavor is appreciated.

leung
gwa
ngau
yuk

凉瓜牛肉

15. CURRY BEEF
Slices of marinated beef are sautéed in oil and curry powder with thick slices of onion, then braised in either beef or chicken broth. If there are six or more people dining, and if most of them like curry, get two orders since this dish disappears very rapidly. It is hot to the taste, but not blazing.

ga
lei
ngau
yuk

咖哩牛肉

16. TOMATOES AND SWEET PEPPERS WITH BEEF
Beef strips sautéed with tomatoes, onions, and green and red peppers, then seasoned with garlic and black bean paste. In most areas this well-flavored dish is best eaten in summer, when the tomatoes and peppers are locally grown.

keh
ju
ngau
yuk

茄椒牛肉

17. BEAN SPROUTS WITH BEEF
Beef slices are sautéed with fresh bean sprouts and ginger root, then lightly braised in soy sauce and wine. The bean sprouts are, of course, still crunchy when served.

nga
choy
ngau
yuk

芽菜牛肉

18. GINGER WITH BEEF

Copious amounts of sliced mature ginger root are braised with beef. Mature ginger is hotter and spicier than young ginger root. Try this during the winter months.

geung

pin

ngau

yuk

19. BEAN THREAD WITH BEEF

Bean thread, another name for cellophane noodles (see Food Notes: Bean Thread), is stir-fried with beef slices, scallions, and Chinese mushrooms. Soy sauce and sherry are usual flavoring additions. This is one of the Cantonese dishes that is "a lot for the money."

fen

see

ngau

yuk

20. CHINESE STRING BEANS WITH BEEF

These unusual, very long string beans, literally "bean corners," are precooked and then sautéed with slices of beef that have been marinated in oyster sauce. Available only in the summer months.

dou

goh

ngau

yuk

21. YOUNG GINGER WITH BEEF

As with most dishes that feature ginger root, this dish is chock-full of the delectable stuff (delectable if you like it). It is sautéed with beef slices, then braised lightly in broth. Available only in spring and early fall.

ji

geung

ngau

yuk

22. LOTUS ROOT WITH BEEF

This delicious nutty "root" is sliced and sautéed with beef, ginger root, wooden ears (tree fungus), and sometimes Chinese celery, then flavored with soy sauce and sherry. Lotus root is generally available from late summer to midwinter.

ling

au

ngau

yuk

23. ASPARAGUS WITH BEEF

Fresh asparagus pieces are braised with sliced beef in soy sauce and brown bean sauce. When properly prepared, the asparagus is crunchy and full-flavored. Available only in season, of course.

lei

sun

ngau

yuk

露笋牛肉

24. BRAISED BEEF (literally "Iron-Pounded Beef")

Flank steak that has been pounded with the flat side of a Chinese cleaver to tenderize it is braised in oyster sauce and a bit of ketchup. A vegetable such as broccoli, *choy sum*, or bean sprouts may be included as well as a topping of crisp rice noodles (not to be confused with chow mein noodles). This is a pleasant, homey dish—rather like Swiss steak.

ti

pa

ngau

yuk

鐵扒牛肉

25. CANTON PRESERVED VEGETABLE WITH BEEF

A spicy, full-flavored dish of sliced beef and thinly shredded preserved vegetable steamed together. The hot-garlicky flavor of the vegetable is quite unusual and may seem too sharp at first taste, but try to work up to it.

chong

choy

ting

ngau

yuk

冲菜蒸牛肉

26. GREEN PEAS WITH CHOPPED BEEF

The peas and meat are stir-fried together, then seasoned with soy sauce and sherry. A simple but enjoyable dish.

ching

dou

ngau

yuk

soong

青豆牛肉鬆

27. FIVE-SPICE BEEF STEW

Beef slices are braised with ginger, oyster sauce, five-spice essence, and sesame oil. Usually served plain (no vegetables), it is a well-flavored, satisfying beef dish.

ng
heung
ngau
nam

五香牛腩

28. FIVE-SPICE BEEF ORGAN MEATS

Various beef organ meats are first tenderized in marinade, then cut up and sautéed with five-spice essence and a few pieces of kidney for flavor. Chopped scallions garnish the top. A bland, unpretentious dish, it tastes best when eaten with a lot of hot-pepper sauce.

ng
heung
ngau
jap

五香牛雜

PORK DISHES

猪　肉　類
jyu　yuk　luy

Note: When the character for meat (肉 , *yuk*) appears alone on the menu, it refers to pork.

1. GREEN (*String*) BEANS WITH PORK

Strips of pork are dry-sautéed with whole beans, bamboo shoots, and mushrooms. The seasoning is just a light touch of sherry. Order in summertime when the beans are fresh and plentiful.

dou
jai
jyu
yuk

豆仔猪肉

2. PORK CAKE

Items *a* through *f* below are all the same dish, topped with different ingredients. The basic ingredient is a large, flat cake made of chopped pork, water chestnuts, soy sauce, sherry, and sometimes ginger. The meat cake is then topped with one of the ingredients listed below, and steamed.

yuk
beun

肉餅

    (a) CHINESE HAM. Slighty salty and hearty but not overpowering.

fo
tuy
yuk
beun

火腿肉餅

    (b) CHINESE SAUSAGE. Unusual flavoring, with a hint of sweetness.

lap
chang
yuk
beun

腊腸肉餅

    (c) PRESERVED KOHLRABI. (*Szechwan Cabbage*). Spicy, salty, and a bit peppery.

jya
choy
yuk
beun

榨菜肉餅

    (d) WINTER VEGETABLE. The taste here is best described as garlicky and salty. Try item *c* before this one.

dung
choy
yuk
beun

冬菜肉餅

(e) SALTED EGG. This specially preserved egg, usually a duck's egg, adds an even stronger and saltier flavor than item *d*.

ham

dan

yuk

beun

(f) SALTED FISH. Delicious in the winter months but quite strong. Not recommended for the neophyte.

ham

yü

yuk

beun

Note: These pork cake dishes are not to be confused with Lion's Head, which is a well-known chopped pork dish in northern Chinese cuisine (see Szechwan Menu: Pork, No. 11). Some northern Chinese restaurants serve the Cantonese pork cake and erroneously call it Lion's Head, but there are differences in the method of preparation.

3. TOMATOES WITH PORK
Slices of fresh pork are braised with fresh tomatoes, scallions, a bit of ginger root, and black bean paste. Best when the tomatoes are in season.

fan

keh

jyu

yuk

4. GREEN PEAS AND CHOPPED PORK
The meat and peas are sautéed together, then flavored with soy sauce, sherry, and ginger root. Enjoyable any time of year.

ching

dou

yuk

soong

5. CANTON PRESERVED VEGETABLE STEAMED WITH PORK

Slices of pork are steamed with this shredded, salted vegetable, which has a strong, fermented flavor. This is a cold-weather dish, and one for educated palates.

chong
choy
ting
yuk
pin

冲菜蒸肉片

6. CHINESE HAM STEAMED WITH FRESH PORK SLICES

This dish is usually seasoned with ginger and garnished with snow peas. Although it's a simple dish, the combination of ham and pork is somewhat unusual to Westerners. Nice in winter.

fo
tuy
ting
yuk
pin

火腿蒸肉片

7. WINTER VEGETABLE (Preserved Celery Cabbage) STEAMED WITH SLICED PORK

The winter vegetable has a strong, garlicky flavor and is delicious when steamed with the pork. Not recommended for beginners.

dung
choy
ting
yuk
pin

冬菜蒸肉片

8. CHOY SUM (Vegetable Heart) WITH PORK

Choy sum is sautéed with pork, scallions, and ginger. Good any time of year for just about any taste preference.

choy
sum
jyu
yuk

菜心猪肉

9. STEAMED CHINESE SAUSAGE

These unusual sausages are served plain here and should be accompanied by some dish containing green vegetables. Sausage dishes should be ordered only during fall and winter months.

ting

lap

chang

蒸腊腸

10. BEAN SPROUTS WITH PORK

This old standby is very good as well as nutritious. Sautéed pork strips are combined with crunchy bean sprouts, a bit of sherry, and soy sauce.

nga

choy

jyu

yuk

芽菜猪肉

11. BEAN CURD WITH PORK

Slices of pork are sautéed with scallions, then braised in oyster sauce with bean curd. The usual addition of a few snow peas provides a nice textural contrast to the bean curd.

dou

fu

jyu

yuk

豆腐猪肉

12. PICKLED MUSTARD GREEN WITH PORK

Slices of pork are sautéed with the pickled greens. Although this is not a very familiar dish to Americans, I can't remember anyone who did not like the sweet-tart flavor of the Chinese mustard pickle.

ham

choy

jyu

yuk

鹹菜猪肉

13. CELLOPHANE NOODLES WITH PORK

Another delicious "lots for the money" dish of fresh pork strips, here sautéed with scallions, bamboo shoots, snow peas, ginger root, and bean thread, then seasoned with sherry and soy sauce.

fen

see

jyu

yuk

粉絲猪肉

Note: Items 14–18 are all dishes combining the well-known *chah shu* (roast pork) with some vegetable. For a general description of roast pork, see Food Notes: Pork, Roast.

14. CHOY SUM (*Vegetable Heart*) WITH ROAST PORK

Slices of the roast pork are lightly braised in broth with *choy sum* and ginger root. A delicate but flavorsome dish.

choy
sum
chah
shu

菜心义燒

15. CHINESE BROCCOLI WITH ROAST PORK

Broccoli is sautéed with sliced roast pork. The rather strong flavor of the broccoli and the barbecued flavor of the pork complement each other nicely.

gai
lan
chah
shu

芥蘭义燒

16. GREEN (*String*) BEANS WITH ROAST PORK

The beans are sautéed with ginger root and sliced pork, then seasoned with soy sauce and sherry. Frozen beans are not used in a Chinese kitchen so this dish is available only during the summer months in most areas.

dou
jai
chah
shu

豆仔义燒

17. SNOW PEAS WITH ROAST PORK

Bamboo shoots, snow peas, and sliced pork are combined, then seasoned with ginger root, soy sauce, and some light dry wine. This is a familiar but always enjoyable dish.

sut
dou
chah
shu

雪豆义燒

18. DICED ROAST PORK
Diced Chinese vegetables such as water chestnuts, ginger root, bamboo shoots, and *bok choy* are sautéed with the pork. Almonds, either whole or slivered, usually garnish the top.

chah

shu

ding

叉燒丁

19. BITTER (*Cool*) MELON WITH PORK
Pieces of fresh pork are braised with melon slices, scallions, garlic, ginger, and black bean paste. Available in summer; not suggested for the uninitiated.

leung

gwa

jyu

yuk

凉瓜猪肉

20. SWEET AND SOUR SPARERIBS
One-inch sections of pork spareribs are browned, then simmered in sweet and pungent sauce.

tim

sün

pai

gwat

甜酸排骨

21. BLACK BEAN SAUCE WITH SPARERIBS
The ribs are cut up and sautéed with black bean sauce, soy sauce, and wine. Black bean sauce itself is made of crushed fermented black beans, ginger, garlic, and scallions.

see

jap

pai

gwat

豉汁排骨

22. FERMENTED BEAN CURD WITH SPARERIBS
This form of bean curd, sometimes called *Chinese cheese* and having the flavor and texture of a rather strong-flavored Camembert, is spooned over sautéed spareribs; *choy sum* is sometimes added. This is a good introduction to the pungent flavor of fermented bean curd.

fu

yü

pai

gwat

付乳排骨

23. SWEET AND SOUR PORK (literally "Sweet and Sour Ancient Old Meat")
A familiar sweet and sour dish, this is made of cubes of pork that are dipped in batter and deep-fried, then combined with onions, sweet peppers, tomatoes, carrots, pineapple, pickled ginger, and frequently sweet mixed pickles.

tim
sün
gu
lo
yuk

24. PLAIN PORK TRIPE
Don't be turned off by any of the tripe dishes in Cantonese cuisine, even though you may usually not care for variety meats. Stir-fried tripe is simmered gently in hot, seasoned broth and served with whatever condiments you desire (soy sauce, oyster sauce, ginger root, pepper sauce).

jing
chō
saang
tou

25. CHOY SUM (*Vegetable Heart*) **WITH PORK TRIPE**
This is a delicately delicious combination of sautéed *choy sum*, tripe, ginger root, and sherry.

choy
sum
saang
tou

26. PRESERVED RED BEAN CURD (literally "Southern Milk") **WITH PIGS' FEET**
This type of bean curd, also called red Chinese cheese, has a flavor similar to that of white preserved bean curd but not so pungent. It is spooned over sautéed pigs' feet that have first been braised with ginger root, sherry, and soy sauce.

nam
yü
jyu
gük

27. CHOY SUM (*Vegetable Heart*) WITH PORK VARIETY MEATS

Pork liver, kidney, and heart are sautéed in a bit of oil with ginger root and *choy sum*, then seasoned with soy sauce and wine. Also very good with some spicy condiment.

choy

sum

jyu

jap

菜心猪雜

28. TEA MELON STEAMED WITH PORK

A delicious and unusual dish of pork strips steamed with tea melon. The flavor of the melon is faintly spicy and sweet.

cha

gwa

ting

jyu

yuk

茶瓜蒸猪肉

29. RED-COOKED SPARERIBS

A mixture of garlic, ginger root, soy sauce, *hoisin* sauce, honey, and sherry is used to marinate the spareribs, which are then roasted until dark reddish brown. They have a wonderful, zesty flavor and are nice as a first course. These are the spareribs most familiar to Westerners, although when served to Chinese, they are cut in small pieces.

hung

shu

pai

gwat

红烧猪骨

30. CHOY SUM (*Vegetable Heart*) WITH SAUSAGE

Choy sum is sautéed with thick slices of Chinese sausage. The crisp vegetable and spicy-sweet sausage are delicious together.

choy

sum

lap

chang

菜心腊腸

31. CHINESE POTATO (*Arrowhead*) WITH SAUSAGE

The white tuber of the arrowhead plant is precooked, then braised with sausage and garnished with fresh coriander. Arrowhead has a mild, nutlike flavor and a mealy texture that absorbs the oiliness of the sausage.

see
gu
lap
chang

茨菇腊腸

32. LOTUS ROOT WITH PORK

Sliced lotus root (or lily root, as it is sometimes called) is sautéed with pork, scallions, and tree ears (tree fungus), then flavored with soy sauce and wine. Everyone likes this crisp "root," which tastes a bit like coconut. It is available from late summer to midwinter.

ling
au
jyu
yuk

蓮藕猪肉

33. BEAN SPROUTS WITH PORK TRIPE

Bean sprouts are sautéed with tripe and seasoned with ginger root and sherry. Try this with a dollop of Chinese mustard.

nga
choy
saang
tou

芽菜生肚

34. ASPARAGUS WITH PORK

Large pieces of fresh asparagus are sautéed with strips of pork, to which are added wine, soy sauce, and oyster sauce. Delightfully fresh and, of course, available only in the asparagus season.

lei
sun
jyu
yuk

露荀猪肉

35. SAUTÉED PORK KIDNEY

A flavorsome dish of sliced kidney with snow peas, bamboo shoots, carrots, and scallions in a zesty sauce flavored with ginger root, soy sauce, pepper, garlic, and sesame oil. If you fancy the French *rognon*, be sure to try this.

chau
yu
fa

炒腰花

36. LITTLE FRY

An extremely pleasant combination of shredded pork, black mushrooms, bean sprouts (both soy and mung), preserved radish, bamboo shoots, golden needles (lily buds), and tree ears (tree fungus), all sautéed together and seasoned with soy sauce and wine. Other ingredients such as shrimp and squid may sometimes be added.

siu

chau

小
炒

SEAFOOD DISHES

海　鮮　類

hoi　sin　luy

1. SAUTÉED FRESH LOBSTER

This authentic Cantonese-style lobster, prepared with scallions, ginger root, minced pork, and black bean paste, is considerably different from and superior to the garlicky, egg-sauced version found on the English-language menu.

chau

lung

ha

炒
龍
蝦

2. PLAIN STEAMED LOBSTER

Lobster is cut up and steamed with scallions and sherry. Sometimes ginger root and soy sauce are added to this delicate but tasty dish.

ching

ting

lung

ha

清
蒸
龍
蝦

3. STUFFED LOBSTER

A whole fresh lobster is steamed after being filled with a luscious stuffing of chopped pork, scallions, water chestnuts, and shrimp, seasoned with ginger root and wine.

yeung

lung

ha

釀
龍
蝦

4. RED-COOKED ABALONE

Sliced abalone, braised lightly in a mixture of soy sauce and oyster sauce, or of soy sauce and *hoisin*, is served on a bed of lettuce with a garnish of chopped peanuts or cashews. Abalone has a pleasant, chewy texture, but should not be rubbery if cooked properly.

hung
shu
bau
yü

5. CHOY SUM (*Vegetable Heart*) WITH SLICED ABALONE

Choy sum is sautéed with thinly sliced abalone, then seasoned with a bit of wine and perhaps some soy sauce. The flavor is subtle and fresh.

choy
sum
bau
pin

Note: The shrimp in dishes 6–8 are cooked and served in the shell. Because of a common Western aversion to picking off the shells, a waiter will sometimes suggest another, similar shrimp dish in which the shrimp are shelled. Despite the effort involved in removing the shells, opt for the "with shell" cooking, since this method really holds the flavor.

6. DRY-PREPARED SHRIMP

This simple dish of lightly browned and delicately seasoned shrimp, always left in the shell, is most enjoyable as a first course. No vegetables are included. "Dry-prepared" simply means that little or no sauce is served with the fish.

gan
jin
ha
luk

7. KETCHUP SHRIMP

Whole shrimp in shell are braised in a tangy sauce of ketchup, soy sauce, and ginger root. A delicious nibble course.

keh
jap
ha
luk

8. BLACK BEAN SAUCE WITH SHRIMP

Whole shrimp in shell are sautéed with black bean paste, ginger root, scallions, garlic, and sherry. The slightly fermented taste of the black bean paste goes well with all shellfish.

see

jap

ha

luk

豉
汁
蝦
碌

9. FU JUNG SHRIMP

This is a thin egg omelette surmounted with sautéed shrimp, scallions, mushrooms, and oyster sauce. All Cantonese *fu jung* dishes are omelettes, combined with various other ingredients—kind of an "Eastern Western."

fu

jung

ha

kao

芙
蓉
蝦
球

10. BEAN CURD WITH SHRIMP

Plain sautéed sliced shrimp are combined with cubes of bean curd and vegetables such as snow peas, scallions, or water chestnuts in a bland, slightly thickened sauce. Usually not a very interesting dish.

dou

fu

ha

pin

豆
腐
蝦
片

11. CHOY SUM (*Vegetable Heart*) WITH SHRIMP

Shrimp, sometimes lightly breaded, are combined with sautéed *choy sum*, snow peas, and water chestnuts, then seasoned with soy sauce and ginger root. Most diners are familiar with this fine dish.

choy

sum

ha

kao

菜
心
蝦
球

12. SWEET AND SOUR SHRIMP

This is another familiar favorite. Whole shrimp are dipped in batter, deep-fried, then served in sweet and sour sauce—usually accompanied by one or more of the following: pineapple chunks, green peppers, loquats, lychees.

tim

sün

ha

kao

甜
酸
蝦
球

13. NEST OF SHRIMP

Large shrimp or prawns are barbecued with bacon strips and beautifully arranged in the shape of a nest on a bed of lettuce. The smoky, barbecued flavor is tantalizing when combined with the sweet-sour sauce that usually accompanies this dish.

wo
tip
ha

窩貼蝦

14. CURRY SHRIMP

A excellent dish of sliced shrimp braised with onions in a Chinese curry sauce. As with other Chinese curries, its spiciness is not incendiary.

ga
lei
ha
pin

咖哩蝦片

15. CHOY SUM (Vegetable Heart) WITH SLICED SHRIMP

A rather simple yet very good combination of *choy sum* sautéed with shrimp and flavored with ginger root, soy sauce, and wine.

choy
sum
ha
pin

菜心蝦片

16. ALMONDS WITH DICED SHRIMP

Almonds, water chestnuts, black mushrooms, and Chinese cabbage (*bok choy*), all diced, are sautéed together with shrimp and snow peas. The usual seasonings are ginger root, garlic, wine, and perhaps a dash of sesame oil.

hang
yan
ha
ding

杏仁蝦丁

17. CELLOPHANE NOODLES AND SHRIMP

Scallions, water chestnuts, snow peas, and sliced shrimp are sautéed together, flavored with ginger root and wine, then combined with the cellophane noodles. Children in particular enjoy eating bean thread since it is so slippery and elusive.

fen
see
ha
pin

粉絲蝦片

18. GREEN PEAS WITH SHRIMP

Whole shelled shrimp, coated with egg white, are deep-fried, then sautéed with scallions, ginger root, and green peas. To be appreciated, the shrimp should be eaten before any full-flavored dishes, as the taste is quite delicate.

ching

dou

ha

yan

19. DEEP-FRIED SHRIMP BOXES (*Shrimp Balls*)

A mixture of raw shrimp chopped together with ginger root and scallions is flavored with a little sherry, then shaped into round "boxes" and deep-fried. These are instant favorites of anyone who tries them. Use plum sauce as a dip.

jau

ha

hop

20. SAUTÉED SLICED TOP SHELL

This unusual mollusk, sautéed in a little oil with *bok choy*, snow peas, and black mushrooms, is lightly seasoned with wine. When top shell is properly prepared, its texture is firm, but not rubbery or tough. Its flavor is fresh and not at all fishy.

chau

heung

lo

pin

21. TOP SHELL WITH CHICKEN

Slices of chicken and top shell are sautéed together with bamboo shoots and *bok choy*, then seasoned with soy sauce and sherry. A fine-flavored, unusual combination.

heung

lo

gai

pin

22. BEAN CURD PAN-FRIED WITH FISH

Sea bass, porgy, or butterfish is first pan-browned, then quickly heated with black bean sauce. The bland bean curd, usually cubed and placed on top, is a nice contrast to the black bean flavor of the fish.

dou

fu

jü

yü

23. RED-COOKED FISH

Whole fish (usually sea bass) is lightly breaded, deep-fried, then gently simmered with minced pork, bamboo shoots, black mushrooms, water chestnuts, and snow peas. Soy sauce, *hoisin*, and ginger root are added for flavor. There are so many ingredients served with the fish that it is almost two dishes in one. Anyone who likes fish will find this dish particularly appealing, even if he has never eaten Chinese food.

hung

shu

yü

紅燒魚

24. WHITE-WATER FISH

A whole water-poached fish (usually sea bass) is served with a delicious garnish of fresh coriander, sliced scallions, bamboo shoots, carrots, and shredded tea melon. This is an exquisite fish dish, worthy of any occasion. (See Chapter 2: Cooking Methods, No. 12.)

bak

sui

yü

白水魚

25. PLAIN SAUTÉED TOP SHELL

Sliced and served on a bed of bean sprouts, watercress, or spinach, the top shell has only the mild flavor of the peanut oil in which it was stir-fried. Sometimes a vague hint of ginger root can be detected.

ching

chō

heung

lo

pin

淨扢响螺片

26. FIVE-STRIPE FISH (Also called *Five-Willow Fish*)

A whole batter-dipped fish (sea bass, grouper, or sole) is deep-fried and served in a luscious sweet-sour sauce. Arranged in stripes across the back are coriander, pickled ginger, sweet peppers, and carrots. The character used here for "stripe" is the same as that used for a particular type of Chinese willow with leaves of such fineness that they resemble lines or stripes. Although Five-Stripe Fish is basically the same as Sweet and Sour Fish, it is considered the more elegant of the two because of its elaborate garnish.

ng

lau

yü

五柳魚

27. SWEET AND SOUR FISH

A whole fish, lightly corn-floured, is deep-fried, then served in a sweet-sour sauce together with ginger root, scallions, onions, carrots, and sweet peppers. Corn-flouring produces a crust that is as delicate as a pastry. Though sea bass is the usual choice for this dish, other fish are used as well.

tim

sün

yü

28. TOMATOES WITH PAN-FRIED FISH

Porgy, butterfish, or sea bass is pan-fried, then combined with tomatoes and black bean sauce. Butterfish is particularly good in this dish.

fan

keh

jü

yü

29. DRIED BEAN CURD WITH PAN-FRIED FISH

A whole pan-fried fish, usually sea bass, is topped with black mushrooms and delicate sheets of dried bean curd, then served in sherried brown bean sauce. Also excellent with butterfish.

yih

juk

jü

yü

30. SAUTÉED FISH SLICES

Fish slices (sole or sea bass) are stir-fried with snow peas, *bok choy*, water chestnuts, and bamboo shoots. Sesame oil adds a pleasant smoky flavor.

chau

yü

pin

31. CHICKEN FAT WITH CARP

Whole carp, brushed with chicken fat, is steamed with ginger root, black mushrooms, scallions, wine, and soy sauce. Since it is quite rich-tasting, carp is usually served as holiday fare among the Cantonese.

gai

yau

li

yü

32. SWEET AND SOUR FISH BITS

Morsels of fresh fish, lightly dipped in batter and deep-fried, are accompanied by snow peas, carrots, and pickled ginger in the sweet and sour sauce. Fish morsels are preferable to a whole sweet-sour fish if fewer than three persons are dining.

tim
sün
yü
kao

甜酸魚球

33. CHOY SUM (*Vegetable Heart*) WITH FISH BITS

Sautéed *choy sum* and water chestnuts are combined with lightly breaded, deep-fried fish chunks in a sauce subtly flavored with sesame oil.

choy
sum
yü
kao

菜心魚球

34. CHOY SUM (*Vegetable Heart*) WITH FISH CAKES

Chopped fish, usually pike, is shaped into cakes that are then sautéed and served with sautéed *choy sum* and oyster sauce. A pleasant, homey dish, it is available in most restaurants only in the fall.

choy
sum
yü
beun

菜心魚餅

35. ONE FISH TWO WAYS

A whole fish is divided and each half is prepared in a different way. For example, half the fish might be sautéed with vegetables and the other half served in sweet-sour sauce, or steamed and garnished with fresh coriander. When this dish is ordered it counts as two.

yat
yü
leung
mei

一魚兩味

36. STEAMED BUTTERFISH

After the entire fish has been steamed, it is garnished with scallions and brown bean sauce. This lovely dish is usually available only in late spring and early summer, but order it whenever possible.

ting
chong
yü

蒸鱠魚

37. SHREDDED PORK WITH STEAMED FLATFISH

Whole flounder or sole, steamed with scallions, ginger root, soy sauce, and sherry, is garnished with sautéed shredded pork and fresh coriander. A marvelous flavor combination, redolent with ginger.

yuk

see

ting

lung

lei

肉絲蒸龍利

38. PLAIN STEAMED FLATFISH

Whole flounder or sole, basically prepared like No. 37, is garnished with preserved kohlrabi (Szechwan cabbage) and shredded ginger. The kohlrabi adds an interesting spiciness.

ching

ting

lung

lei

清蒸龍利

39. SAUTÉED CHOPPED DRIED OYSTERS

Dried oysters chopped with pork, bamboo shoots, green peas, mushrooms, and water chestnuts are sautéed and served plain. This is a fairly rich dish that should be accompanied by a leafy vegetable or something tart.

chau

ho

see

soong

炒蠔豉鬆

40. DEEP-FRIED FRESH OYSTERS

Oysters that have been marinated in ginger root and onion juices are lightly breaded, deep-fried, and served with little side dishes of sauce. Try these luscious morsels even if you don't like oysters.

jau

saang

ho

炸生蠔

41. RED-COOKED CRAB

Cut-up crab is braised in soy sauce together with scallions, black bean paste, and ginger root. The black bean flavor is quite concentrated, since very little liquid is added during braising. Perfect as an appetizer.

hung

shu

hai

紅燒蟹

42. OYSTER SAUCE WITH SAUTÉED CLAMS

Clams in the shell are first stir-fried, then braised in oyster sauce with scallions. The clam broth blends with the oyster sauce to make a superb gravy.

ho
yau
chau
heen
蠔油炒蜆

43. SWEET AND SOUR SAUTÉED CLAMS

Most Westerners are not familiar with clams served in sweet and pungent sauce. The clams are prepared in shell. This dish is particularly good when the clams are small.

tim
sün
chau
heen
甜酸炒蜆

44. BLACK BEAN SAUCE AND SAUTÉED CLAMS

Black bean paste, ginger, garlic, scallions, and wine are added to sautéed clams in the shell, which then are simmered just long enough to absorb the deep, pungent black bean flavor.

see
jap
chau
heen
豉汁炒蜆

45. BATTER-DIPPED OYSTERS

Deep-fried oysters that have first been dipped in a delicate, puffy batter are combined with bamboo shoots, *choy sum*, and oyster sauce. This is a marvelous seafood dish.

saang
gan
saang
ho
生狠生蠔

46. SAUTÉED CRAB WITH CRAB ROE

A whole crab with its roe is cut up and sautéed with scallions, ginger root, and black bean paste, then combined with scrambled eggs. A rich-tasting dish, it is available only in winter, when crabs are carrying roe.

chau
go
hai
炒羔蟹

47. CRAB MEAT WITH MUSHROOMS

Mushrooms, usually the straw or button variety, are stir-fried with scallions, ginger root, soy sauce, sherry, and crabmeat. A lovely, delicate dish.

hai
yuk
bat
sin
gu

蟹肉扒鮮菇

48. DEEP-FRIED FRESH CRAB CLAWS

A delectable first course, especially for seafood lovers. Shelled crab claws, lightly dipped in seasoned batter, are deep-fried and served with lemon wedges.

jau
sin
hai
kin

炸鮮蟹鉗

49. SAUTÉED ROCK SNAILS

Rock snails are the little blue-black marine snails commonly known as periwinkles. Quite different in taste from the French *escargots*, these rock snails are prepared in a devilishly divine spicy sauce of garlic, red pepper, ginger root, scallions, and black bean paste. They make an excellent first course. Be sure to ask the waiter how to get them out of their shells; there's a neat little trick to it.

chau
syet
lo

炒石螺

50. PLAIN FRESH SQUID

Squid is cooked in hot broth faintly flavored with sesame oil and served on a bed of bean sprouts, spinach, or watercress. This simple but appealing squid dish is typical of Cantonese culinary skill.

chō
sin
yau

泃鮮魷

51. SAUTÉED FRESH SQUID

Cut-up fresh squid is sautéed with garlic, ginger root, scallions, and bamboo shoots. Green peppers are sometimes added, and sesame oil is used as seasoning. This is a savory dish that even non-squid eaters will relish.

chau
sin
yau

炒鮮魷

52. PLAIN DRIED SQUID

Squid is braised in oyster sauce and light soy sauce with just enough Chinese celery, scallions, and ginger root for flavor, then served on a bed of lettuce. Dried squid has a pleasant smoky flavor.

chō

ying

yau

托英魷

53. SAUTÉED DRIED SQUID

Choy sum, bamboo shoots, and ginger root are sautéed with dried squid to make this hearty, full-flavored dish. Oyster sauce and light soy accent the flavors.

chau

ying

yau

炒英魷

54. BATTER-DIPPED FROGS' LEGS

Small frogs' legs are lightly breaded, braised, and seasoned with black bean paste, garlic, ginger root, and wine. A wonderful and savory dish, it is much more delicate than the French version. Cantonese use the expression "field chicken" for edible frogs.

saang

gen

mun

tin

gai

生狼牧田鶏

55. KING CRAB WITH SAUTÉED SHREDDED SHARK'S FIN

Crab meat, shark's fin, and beaten eggs are stir-fried together, then seasoned with sesame oil. Since all shark's fin dishes are considered delicacies and since the shark's fin itself is quite costly, this is a very expensive dish.

hai

wang

chau

jih

蟹王炒翅

56. SAUTÉED THREE-INGREDIENT SEAFOOD DISH

Fish, shrimp, and chunks of sautéed lobster are combined with black mushrooms and such Chinese vegetables as *choy sum* and snow peas to make a toothsome but rather expensive dish. (This is similar to No. 57, but simpler.)

chau

sam

sin

炒三鮮

57. Sautéed Eight-Ingredient Seafood Dish

An elaborate mélange of sautéed lobster, shrimp, fish, abalone, sea cucumber, and other "fruits of the sea." Snow peas, bamboo shoots, water chestnuts, and *bok choy* are usually included. The high cost of the ingredients makes this dish quite expensive.

chau

bat

sin

58. Cassia Flower Sautéed Shark's Fin

Chopped pork, shark's fin, and bean sprouts are combined with scrambled eggs, then delicately seasoned with light soy sauce and sesame oil to make this delicious and elegant dish, which, like No. 55, is very expensive. The fanciful name is meant to describe the appearance of the dish when it is served.

gwai

fa

chau

jih

59. Red-Cooked Sea Cucumber

Sea cucumber (*bêche-de-mer*) is highly esteemed as a delicacy in Chinese cuisine, but Westerners may find it too soft and strange-tasting at first. This dish is made of sea cucumber braised in a mixture of soy sauce, scallions, ginger root, and sherry. Sliced bamboo shoots add a nice textural contrast.

hung

shu

hoi

sum

VEGETABLE DISHES

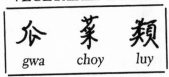

gwa choy luy

1. Sautéed Chinese Broccoli

This hearty-flavored vegetable is sautéed briefly and seasoned with a bit of sesame oil. Try it with an order of plain, sliced roast pork.

chau

gai

lan

2. SAUTÉED CHOY SUM (*Vegetable Heart*)

Ginger root and sesame oil are the usual flavorings for sautéed *choy sum*, a delicate member of the cabbage family.

chau
choy
sum

炒菜心

3. SAUTÉED MUSTARD GREENS

This pungent vegetable is best eaten with dishes that have pronounced flavors but not with very bland ones. Soy Sauce Chicken (No. 30) is one good choice.

chau
gai
choy

炒芥菜

4. SAUTÉED MIXED VEGETABLES

Although the vegetable combination depends upon the chef, it usually consists of such Oriental and Western vegetables as *bok choy*, water chestnuts, tomatoes, bamboo shoots, sweet peppers, and tiny ears of corn.

chau
sap
choy

炒什菜

5. SAUTÉED BEAN SPROUTS

A simple but very good dish that combines sautéed mung bean sprouts, scallions, ginger root, soy sauce, and a little wine. The bean sprouts should be still crunchy when served.

chau
nga
choy

炒芽菜

6. ARHAT'S FEAST (*Monk's Food*)

Here is an extravagant vegetarian combination of lotus root, lily buds, gingko nuts, bamboo shoots, wooden ears (tree fungus), black mushrooms, hair seaweed, dried bean curd, and fermented bean curd. Dried bean curd is the ingredient that has the appearance and taste of meat (without the cholesterol). There are some unusual flavors in Arhat's Feast that you may not appreciate at first; be assured, however, that it is worth at least one more try. This dish is also known as *lo han chai* and Buddha's Delight.

lo
han
chai

羅漢齋

7. FERMENTED BEAN CURD WITH STRING BEANS

Sautéed fresh green beans (usually whole) are tossed with white fermented bean curd, which tastes like a sour-cream dressing in this dish.

fu
yü
dou
jai

腐乳豆仔

8. FERMENTED BEAN CURD WITH LETTUCE

Slightly wilted lettuce (usually romaine) is mixed with white fermented bean curd, whose strong "cheesy" flavor is excellent with the delicate taste of the romaine.

fu
yü
saang
choy

腐乳生菜

9. FERMENTED BEAN CURD WITH WATERCRESS

The two ingredients are very briefly heated so as to preserve the distinctive texture and flavor of the cress. Refreshing on a hot day when accompanied by some milder dish.

fu
yü
sai
yang
choy

腐乳西洋菜

10. STUFFED BITTER MELON

Although this is not strictly a vegetable dish, I have included it with my selection of vegetable dishes because the melon is the prominent ingredient. A subtly seasoned mixture of chopped shrimp, pork, and fish is used to fill the scooped-out melon, which is then baked in a sauce of ginger, scallions, soy sauce, and black bean paste. Because of its unusual flavor I suggest that one of the simpler bitter melon dishes (bitter melon with pork or beef, for example) be tried before this one.

yeung
fu
gwa

釀苦瓜

11. OYSTER SAUCE WITH BROCCOLI HEART

Heart of Chinese broccoli is stir-fried with ginger root, then braised in oyster sauce. Its full flavor and crunchy texture make this a very satisfying vegetable dish.

ho

yau

gai

sum

蠔油蘭心

12. CHICKEN FAT BRAISED BLACK MUSHROOMS

As simple as this dish sounds—nothing else is included —it is truly fine fare, but also expensive because black mushrooms are costly.

gai

yau

dung

gu

鷄油冬菇

13. FERMENTED BEAN CURD WITH SPINACH

Spinach is briefly sautéed in oil, then mixed with fermented bean curd, which is also called Chinese cheese. Although the flavor of this "cheese" is strong, the spinach somewhat diminishes its sharpness.

fu

yü

bo

choy

腐乳菠菜

EGG DISHES

蛋 類

dan   *luy*

All of the stirred (scrambled) egg dishes below (Nos. 1–5) are combinations of eggs and fish or meat plus scallions, ginger root, green peas, bamboo shoots,

mushrooms, and water chestnuts. A light covering of
oyster sauce usually accompanies these dishes. Egg
dishes add variety to a menu without being too filling.

1. FRESH SHRIMP WITH STIRRED EGGS

sin

ha

chau

dan

2. FLAKED FISH WITH STIRRED EGGS

yü

yuk

chau

dan

3. CHINESE HAM WITH STIRRED EGGS

fo

tuy

chau

dan

4. ROAST PORK WITH STIRRED EGGS

chah

shu

chau

dan

5. BEEF WITH STIRRED EGGS

ngau

yuk

chau

dan

牛肉炒蛋

6. PICKLED GINGER WITH PRESERVED EGGS

These are the famous jewel-like Thousand-Year-Old Eggs. Pickled ginger root and scallions, which offset the richness of the eggs, are the usual condiments served with these unusual delicacies. Preserved eggs should be sampled sparingly, since their rather strong, sulfurous flavor and brilliant color are very alien to most Westerners.

sün

geung

pei

dan

酸薑皮蛋

BEAN CURD DISHES

豆　腐　類

dou　fu　luy

1. OYSTER SAUCE WITH BEAN CURD

Made simply with scallions and oyster sauce, this dish is a pleasant accompaniment for plain roast pork or just a dish of vegetables.

ho

yau

dou

fu

蠔油豆腐

2. DEEP-FRIED BEAN CURD

Triangular pieces of bean curd are deep-fried and served with oyster sauce, soy sauce, scallions, and usually a few snow peas. The texture of deep-fried bean curd is much firmer than that of plain bean curd.

jau

dou

fu

炸豆腐

3. RED-COOKED BEAN CURD

Bean curd is gently braised with bits of pork, black mushrooms, bamboo shoots, scallions, and soy sauce. This is a very nice dish for people not quite accustomed to the blandness of bean curd.

hung

shu

dou

fu

紅燒豆腐

4. COLD SLICED BEAN CURD

This refreshing summer dish, served with condiments of sesame oil or soy sauce, goes well with most dishes, hot or cold. Try it with White Cut Chicken (Chicken, No. 35).

leung

ban

dou

fu

凉辦豆腐肉

5. STUFFED BEAN CURD

Squares of bean curd are stuffed with a tempting mixture of chopped pork, shrimp, fish, scallions, sherry, and soy sauce, then steamed. Sprigs of fresh coriander, soy sauce, and sherry accompany this *haute cuisine* bean curd dish.

yeung

dou

fu

釀豆腐

POTTED RICE

煲	飯	類
bo	fan	luy

Bo fan, which literally means "potted rice," is a simple, almost rustic dish that originally was prepared in an earthenware pot. Although most restaurants now use metalware, the cooking procedure is much the same. White rice and water are boiled together until the rice is partially cooked. Then pieces of sausage, beef, or other meat with some added flavorings are placed on top of the rice, which absorbs the flavors of the added ingredients during the final minutes of cooking. The dish is served in its cooking vessel. An added treat, after the rice is eaten, is the brown crust that has formed at the bottom of the pot. This is customarily eaten after it has first been softened with hot water.

Potted rice dishes, available only in autumn and winter, take the place of the usual bowls of rice that accompany the meal. One rice pot is more than adequate for four persons.

1. CHINESE SAUSAGE WITH POTTED RICE
Large slices of sausage are steamed on top of white rice. This aromatic, slightly sweet sausage has a firm, pepperoni-like texture. You might also ask the waiter to add a few slices of duck liver sausage (鴨 肝 腸 opp gan chong).

lap 腊
chang 腸
bo 煲
fan 飯

2. BEEF WITH POTTED RICE
Strips of beef are steamed with ginger root on top of white rice. A few pieces of scallion are sometimes added.

ngau 牛
yuk 肉
bo 煲
fan 飯

3. CHICKEN WITH POTTED RICE

Pieces of chicken (bone in) that have been marinated in soy and wine are steamed with white rice. Ginger root and scallions are often added.

gai

luk

bo

fan

鷄
碌
煲
飯

4. CHICKEN MORSELS WITH POTTED RICE

Chunks of chicken, flavored with soy sauce and sometimes wine and ginger root, are steamed with white rice.

gai

kao

bo

fan

鷄
球
煲
飯

5. SQUAB WITH POTTED RICE

Cut-up squab, seasoned with dark soy sauce and sometimes dried orange peel, is steamed with white rice.

bak

kap

bo

fan

白
鴿
煲
飯

4

ORdERiNG
fROM THE CANTONESE MENU

The Cantonese menu is extensive, and the effect of it can be staggering on first contact. A friend of mine, upon seeing the menu in this guide, remarked that it made him feel like a child in a candy store; he wanted to try one of everything immediately. While there seems to be a real temptation to do just this, some degree of prudence and forbearance is recommended. It is permissible, in fact almost obligatory, to take leftovers with you when you leave a Cantonese restaurant, but it is better not to overorder. So the disposition of the dining party's collective appetite should be determined beforehand. Try to gauge the selection toward the average taste and capacity of the group. If in a party of four, for example, there are two small appetites, it is preferable to order three dishes and soup rather than the one dish per person plus soup suggested below. If some members of the party are cautious in their tastes, don't order too many things that might jar the naïve palate. But if someone in the party wants to combine the authentic Chinese viands with some of his clichéed favorites, such as shrimp with lobster sauce, you would do best to ask him to stay at home; he will undermine your credibility as a serious diner.

It is often alleged that dishes on the Chinese menu are less expensive than the same ones on the English menu. Ostensibly, this is indeed the case; but don't attribute it to any discriminatory practice. Westerners habitually demand more meat in their dishes, and also expect larger portions, since many are not accustomed to the Chinese preference for taking a little from numerous dishes of smaller portions. When dinner is ordered from the Chinese-language menu in a Cantonese restaurant the price is almost invariably a pleasant surprise. It makes the patron realize why Chinese food is considered one of the few legitimate bargains still to be found. For the curious, the Chinese characters for prices as they appear on the Chinese menu are given in the Appendix.

For convenience and clarity, pointers on ordering are listed below:

1. A good general rule to follow is to allow one dish per person plus soup.
2. If you want a fish course and only two persons are dining, it is better to have fish bits with vegetables than to order a whole fish.
3. If more than six people are dining together, ordering double portions of some dishes is often preferable to ordering single portions of several dishes.
4. If the party is large, include a "nibble course" such as snails or shrimp boxes and order as wide a variety of foods as possible—fowl, beef, pork, seafood, and so on.
5. Order a good representation of dishes and flavors for the number of people present. If four people are dining together, don't ask for two shellfish dishes, or two that are made with black bean sauce.
6. Consider textures and sizes of food pieces. If soup with bean curd is ordered, don't order another bean curd dish unless the dining party is large.
7. Make certain that some green vegetable is included among your selections. If none of the dishes is prepared with a green, ask for a soup made with one.
8. When making menu decisions, try to be sure that what you are ordering is in season. Don't accept a canned or dried substitute, such as canned bitter melon, for fresh. The reader should be aware, however, that some dishes are made only with a dried or canned product because the recipe may specifically require its use, or because certain items such as straw mushrooms are almost never available fresh. Seasonal dishes are often indicated in the listings of this chapter. If there are doubts, ask the waiter.
9. Sweet and sour dishes are not eaten nearly so frequently by the Chinese as by Westerners, even though they are found on the Chinese menu. Lest you and your party be associated with the "sweet and sour syndrome," refrain from ordering one of these dishes unless there is a sufficient number of other selections (five or six) to balance the sweet-sour one.

5

========= ● ========= ● ========= ● =========

SAMPLE CANTONESE dINNERS

Sample dinners for two, three or four, and six people are given in the following pages. There are choices to suit different tastes and levels of sophistication—Curious, Knowledgeable, and Adventurous. The Chinese characters for the different dishes are written vertically from top to bottom, as they appear on an actual Cantonese menu, and the dishes are listed from right to left beginning with the soup. All the dinners have been seasonally coordinated, which means that a dish made with a vegetable available only in the spring has not been placed with a dish made with winter ingredients. Much of the information pertaining to seasonally available foods can be found in the menu descriptions of this guide, but if in doubt, ask the waiter.

Select a dinner that is appropriate to the size and taste of your dining party. If one or more of the dishes is unavailable, ask the waiter for suitable substitutes, or use the guide's Cantonese Menu itself.

To find descriptions of the dishes given in the sample dinners, note the section (italics) and number (Arabic numerals) of the selections as they appear in the Cantonese Menu. Thus, for example, "(4) Bean Curd *Soup*" will tell you that the dish is described in the Soup section of the Cantonese Menu, and that it is item No. 4.

FOR TWO PEOPLE

curious	knowledgeable	adventurous
18/Green Pea and Diced Chicken Soup	11/Watercress Soup	8/Seaweed Soup
7/Choy Sum with Beef	19/Tomatoes with Chicken (Fowl)	7/Sautéed Minced Young Squab (Fowl)
41/Deep-Fried Chicken Wings (Fowl)	13/Cellophane Noodles with Pork	12/Pickled Mustard Green with Pork

curious

15/Tomato Egg-Flower Soup

10/Bean Sprouts with Pork

33/Choy Sum with Fish Bits (Seafood)

蕃 茄 蛋 湯

豆 芽 炒 肉

雜 菜 猪 花 湯
球 肉 湯

knowledgeable

6/Clear Broth with Seasonal Vegetable (Soup)

36/Little Fry (Pork)

5/Choy Sum with Sliced Abalone
(Seafood)

菜 小 清
心 湯
鮑 炒 時
片 菜 湯

adventurous

10/Black Mushroom and Abalone
Soup

5/Preserved Kohlrabi Steamed with
Beef

34/Asparagus with Pork

蘆 冬 北
筍 菜 菇
肉 蒸 鮑
肉 牛 魚
湯

SAMPLE CANTONESE DINNERS

curious	knowledgeable	adventurous
4/Bean Curd Soup	5/Chicken Velvet and Sweet Corn Soup	20/Sliced Fresh Pork and Mustard Green Soup
23/Almonds with Diced Chicken (Fowl)	2/Chinese Broccoli with Beef	32/Curry Chicken (Fowl)
15/Choy Sum with Sliced Shrimp (Seafood)	16/Almonds with Diced Shrimp (Seafood)	42/Oyster Sauce with Sautéed Clams (Seafood)

菜 杏 豆
心 仁 腐
蝦 雞 湯
片 丁 湯

杏 芥 雞
仁 蘭 茸
蝦 牛 粟
丁 肉 米
湯

蠔 咖 肉
油 哩 片
炒 雞 芥
蜆 嗲 菜
湯

IV **curious**

6/Clear Broth with Seasonal Vegetable (*Soup*)

11/*Choy Sum* with Chicken Morsels
(*Fowl*)

16/Tomato and Sweet Peppers with
Beef

knowledgeable

22/Sour and Hot *Soup*

9/*Crisp Fried Chicken*

17/Cellophane Noodles and Shrimp
(*Seafood*)

adventurous

1/Chicken Velvet and Shark's Fin
Soup

45/Golden Needle *Chicken Wings*

8/Fermented Bean Curd with Lettuce (*Vegetables*)

V curious

12/Hair Melon *Soup*

9/Crisp Fried *Chicken*

3/Tomatoes with *Pork*

冬　茄子猪　　炸鷄　　瓜　　肉　　湯

knowledgeable

13/Fish Slices and Lettuce in Clear Broth (*Soup*)

26/Ham with Sliced *Chicken*

3/Sautéed Mustard Greens (*Vegetables*)

炒火生芥腿菜鷄魚片菜片湯

adventurous

17/Sea Cucumber and Abalone *Soup*

3/Lemon Squab (*Fowl*)

16/Green Beans with Roast *Pork*

豆輝海芽汁鮑又白魚燒鴿湯

VI

curious	knowledgeable	adventurous
4/Bean Curd Soup	16/Clear Simmered Mushrooms (Soup)	5/Chicken Velvet and Sweet Corn Soup
22/Walnuts with Diced Chicken (Fowl)	32/Curry Chicken (Fowl)	50/Heart of Choy Sum with Duck (Fowl)
3/Pickled Mustard Green with Beef	7/Choy Sum with Beef	5/Preserved Kohlrabi Steamed with Beef

VII

curious

18/Green Pea and Diced Chicken Soup

53/Chinese Mushrooms with Duck (*Fowl*)

8/*Choy Sum* with *Pork*

荣心豬肉
北菇扒鴨
青豆雞
菜遠湯

knowledgeable

4/Bean Curd Soup

20/Chinese Mushrooms Steamed with Chicken (*Fowl*)

2/Chinese Broccoli with Beef

芥蘭牛肉
北菇蒸雞
豆腐湯

adventurous

21/Ridged Melon Soup with Straw Mushrooms and Bean Curd

35/White Cut Chicken (*Fowl*)

21/Young Ginger with Beef

子匀
毛切牛肉
介鷄
草菇
勝豆腐湯

VIII

curious	knowledgeable	adventurous
5/Chicken Velvet and Sweet Corn *Soup*	12/Hair Melon *Soup*	7/Clear Broth with Fish Dumpling (*Soup*)
1/Sautéed *Beef* Cubes	37/Satellite Chicken (*Fowl*)	1/Crisp Fried Squab (*Fowl*)
11/*Choy Sum* with Shrimp (*Seafood*)	45/Batter-dipped Oysters (*Seafood*)	15/Chinese Broccoli with Roast Pork

IX curious

23/Bottle Gourd Melon *Soup*

18/Oyster Sauce with Chicken (*Fowl*)

3/Pickled Mustard Green with *Beef*

鹹蝦瓜湯

蠔油滑雞

汁雞片

肉辣湯

knowledgeable

14/Pickled Mustard Green and Bean Curd *Soup*

42/Lemon Chicken Wings (*Fowl*)

8/Mushrooms with *Beef* Cubes

鮮菰鼓試

汁菇菜

市雞豆

的翼滿

球湯

adventurous

9/Ham and Mustard Green *Soup*

33/Young Ginger with Sliced Chicken (*Fowl*)

51/Sautéed Fresh Squid (*Seafood*)

炒子火

鮮薑腿

魷雞芥

片菜

湯

adventurous

16/Clear Simmered Mushrooms (*Soup*)

12/Bitter Melon with Chicken Chunks (*Fowl*)

24/White-Water Fish (*Seafood*)

knowledgeable

20/Sliced Fresh Pork and Mustard Green *Soup*

46/Three-Ingredient Roast Duck (*Fowl*)

28/Tomatoes with Pan-Fried Fish (*Seafood*)

X curious

13/Fish Slices and Lettuce in Clear Broth (*Soup*)

24/Green Peas with Diced Chicken (*Fowl*)

13/Cellophane Noodles with *Pork*

XI

curious	knowledgeable	adventurous
15/Tomato Egg-Flower Soup	11/Watercress Soup	8/Seaweed Soup
36/Fresh Mushrooms and Chicken (*Fowl*)	13/Lobster and Chicken Chunks (*Fowl*)	31/Fresh Ginger Root with Braised Chicken (*Fowl*)
11/Snow Peas with Beef	16/Green Beans with Roast Pork	2/Chinese Broccoli with Beef

XII

curious

12/Hair Melon Soup

43/Ketchup Chicken Wings (*Fowl*)

26/Green Peas with Chopped *Beef*

knowledgeable

1/Chicken Velvet and Shark's Fin Soup

39/Chicken Livers with Sliced Chicken (*Fowl*)

4/Sautéed Mixed *Vegetables*

adventurous

11/Watercress Soup

14/Bitter Melon with *Beef*

3/Red-Cooked *Bean Curd*

XIII

curious

4/Bean Curd Soup

29/Asparagus and Sliced Chicken (*Fowl*)

20/Sweet and Sour Spareribs (*Pork*)

甜酸排骨
鹹爽蘆筍雞片
湯

knowledgeable

22/Sour and Hot Soup

15/Ham with Steamed Chicken (*Fowl*)

11/Oyster Sauce with Broccoli Heart (*Vegetables*)

蠔油腿蘭
火腿蒸雞
酸辣湯
心

adventurous

17/Sea Cucumber and Abalone Soup

16/Sausage Steamed with Chicken (*Fowl*)

1/Sautéed Chinese Broccoli (*Vegetables*)

炒腊海
芥腊參
蘭蒸鮑
雞魚
湯

XIV

curious

18/Green Pea and Diced Chicken Soup

47/Sautéed Shredded Roast Duck (Fowl)

15/Choy Sum with Sliced Shrimp (Seafood)

knowledgeable

23/Bottle Gourd Melon Soup

30/Soy Sauce Chicken (Fowl)

5/Sautéed Bean Sprouts (Vegetables)

adventurous

13/Fish Slices and Lettuce in Clear Broth (Soup)

17/Black Bean Sauce with Chicken (Fowl)

10/Winter Vegetable Steamed with Beef

XV curious

23/Bottle Gourd Melon Soup

25/Snow Peas with Sliced Chicken
(*Fowl*)

4/Oyster Sauce with Beef

knowledgeable

7/Clear Broth with Fish Dumplings
(*Soup*)

34/Lotus Root and Sliced Chicken
(*Fowl*)

2/Sautéed Choy Sum (*Vegetables*)

adventurous

21/Ridged Melon *Soup* with Straw
Mushrooms and Bean Curd

10/Fresh Fish and Chicken Morsels
(*Fowl*)

21/Black Bean Sauce with Spareribs
(*Pork*)

FOR THREE OR FOUR PEOPLE

curious

13/Fish Slices and Lettuce in Clear Broth (*Soup*)

25/Snow Peas with Sliced Chicken (*Fowl*)

2a/Pork Cake with Chinese Ham

1/Fresh Shrimp with Stirred *Eggs*

knowledgeable

9/Ham and Mustard Green *Soup*

1/Crisp Fried Squab (*Fowl*)

32/Lotus Root with Pork

2/Sautéed Choy Sum (*Vegetables*)

adventurous

7/Clear Broth with Fish Dumpling (*Soup*)

12/Bitter Melon with Chicken Chunks (*Fowl*)

13/Fermented Bean Curd with Spinach (*Vegetables*)

4/Green Peas and Chopped *Pork*

curious

23/Bottle Gourd Melon *Soup*

13/Lobster and Chicken Chunks (*Fowl*)

16/Tomatoes and Sweet Peppers with *Beef*

1/Green Beans with *Pork*

knowledgeable

16/Clear-Simmered Mushrooms (*Soup*)

16/Sausage Steamed with Chicken (*Fowl*)

3/Pickled Mustard Green with *Beef*

8/Black Bean Sauce with Shrimp (*Seafood*)

adventurous

21/Ridged Melon *Soup* with Straw Mushrooms and Bean Curd

52/Roast Duck (*Fowl*)

9/Soured Bamboo Shoots Steamed with *Beef*

23/Red-Cooked Fish (*Seafood*)

▌▌▌

curious

6/Clear Broth with Seasonal Vegetable (*Soup*)

9/Crisp Fried Chicken (*Fowl*)

18/Green Peas with Shrimp (*Seafood*)

14/*Choy Sum* with Roast Pork

knowledgeable

12/Hair Melon Soup

46/Three-Ingredient Roast Duck (*Fowl*)

24/White-Water Fish (*Seafood*)

1/Sautéed Chinese Broccoli (*Vegetables*)

adventurous

17/Sea Cucumber and Abalone *Soup*

42/Lemon Chicken Wings (*Fowl*)

2d/Pork Cake with Winter Vegetable

3/Red-Cooked Bean Curd

adventurous

15/Tomato Egg-Flower Soup

31/Fresh Ginger Root with Braised
Chicken (Fowl)

5/Canton Preserved Vegetable
Steamed with Pork

11/Snow Peas with Beef

番

茄

滚

蛋

湯

生

薑

蒸

焗

肉

片

雪

冲

豆

牛

肉

knowledgeable

7/Clear Broth with Fish Dumpling
(Soup)

43/Ketchup Chicken Wings (Fowl)

15/Chinese Broccoli with Roast Pork

2/Flaked Fish with Stirred Eggs

清

湯

魚

介

茄

汁

肉

翅

叉

鷄

品

炒

鷄

蛋

及

第

魚

湯

IV curious

4/Bean Curd Soup

1/Crisp Fried Squab (Fowl)

1/Green Beans with Pork

16/Almonds with Diced Shrimp
(Seafood)

杏

仁

炸

猪

蝦

豆

乳

鴿

肉

仁

豆

腐

湯

V curious

6/Clear Broth with Seasonal Vegetable (Soup)

24/Green Peas with Diced Chicken (Fowl)

8/Mushrooms with Beef Cubes

14/Choy Sum with Roast Pork

knowledgeable

22/Sour and Hot Soup

9/Crisp Fried Chicken (Fowl)

2/Chinese Broccoli with Beef

23/Sweet and Sour Pork

adventurous

10/Black Mushroom and Abalone Soup

14/Steamed Salt Chicken (Fowl)

16/Green Beans with Roast Pork

8/Black Bean Sauce with Shrimp (Seafood)

VI curious

18/Green Pea and Diced Chicken Soup

50/Heart of Choy Sum with Duck (Fowl)

10/Bean Sprouts with Pork

6/Dry-Prepared Shrimp (Seafood)

青豆雞茸湯

鴨腳扣菜膽

豬肉炒芽菜

乾煎蝦碌鴨湯

knowledgeable

23/Bottle Gourd Melon Soup

34/Lotus Root and Sliced Chicken (Fowl)

36/Little Fry (Pork)

16/Tomatoes and Sweet Peppers with Beef

節瓜小魚湯

蓮藕雞片

小炒

牛肉炒番茄

adventurous

14/Pickled Mustard Green and Bean Curd Soup

35/White Cut Chicken (Fowl)

7/Winter Vegetable Steamed with Sliced Pork

1/Fresh Shrimp with Stirred Eggs

鹹菜豆腐湯

白切雞

冬菜蒸肉片

鮮蝦炒蛋

VII

curious	knowledgeable	adventurous
12/Hair Melon Soup	13/Fish Slices and Lettuce in Clear Broth (*Soup*)	8/Seaweed Soup
20/Chinese Mushrooms Steamed with Chicken (*Fowl*)	19/Tomatoes with Chicken (*Fowl*)	17/Black Bean Sauce with Chicken (*Fowl*)
4/Green Peas and Chopped Pork	11/Bean Curd with Pork	32/Lotus Root with Pork
30/Sautéed Fish Slices (*Seafood*)	15/Choy Sum with Sliced Shrimp (*Seafood*)	5/Choy Sum with Sliced Abalone (*Seafood*)

VIII

curious

23/Bottle Gourd Melon Soup

44/Oyster Sauce Chicken Wings (*Fowl*)

8/Choy Sum with Pork

10/Bean Curd with Shrimp (*Seafood*)

冬瓜湯

蠔油雞翼

油菜心

蝦仁豆腐

knowledgeable

14/Pickled Mustard Green and Bean Curd Soup

53/Chinese Mushrooms with Duck (*Fowl*)

17/Snow Peas with Roast Pork

17/Cellophane Noodles and Shrimp (*Seafood*)

鹹酸菜豆腐湯

北菇燜鴨

荷蘭豆叉燒肉片

蝦仁粉絲

adventurous

3/Sliced Chicken and Shark's Fin Soup

30/Soy Sauce Chicken (*Fowl*)

2f/Pork Cake and Salted Fish

11/Oyster Sauce with Broccoli Heart (*Vegetables*)

雞絲魚翅

豉油雞

鹹魚肉餅

蠔油芥蘭

IX

curious

15/Tomato Egg-Flower Soup

11/*Choy Sum* with Chicken Morsels (*Fowl*)

18/Diced Roast *Pork*

18/Green Peas with Shrimp (*Seafood*)

青 火 菜 湯
豆 燒 心 加
蝦 丁 雞 蛋
仁 球 花
湯

knowledgeable

16/Clear-Simmered Mushrooms (*Soup*)

47/Sautéed Shredded Roast Duck (*Fowl*)

28/Tea Melon Steamed with *Pork*

3/Sautéed Mustard Greens (*Vegetables*)

竹 茶 竹 清
笋 瓜 火 燉
炒 蒸 鴨 北
菜 腊 絲 菇
肉

adventurous

22/Sour and Hot Soup

16/Sausage Steamed with Chicken (*Fowl*)

19/Bitter Melon with *Pork*

25/Plain Sautéed Top Shell (*Seafood*)

清 涼 腊 酸
炒 瓜 腸 辣
響 炒 蒸 湯
螺 肉 雞
片

X curious

5/Chicken Velvet and Sweet Corn Soup

41/Deep-Fried Chicken Wings (*Fowl*)

7/Choy Sum with Beef

12/Sweet and Sour Shrimp (*Seafood*)

甜粟米雞蓉湯
炸雞心翼
蝦炒菜遠
甜酸蜜汁蝦肉球湯

knowledgeable

11/Watercress Soup

18/Oyster Sauce with Chicken (*Fowl*)

6/Ham Steamed with Beef

4/Sautéed Mixed Vegetables

炒火鴨西洋菜
蠔油蒸雞
竹蒸牛肉
炒什菜遠湯

adventurous

7/Clear Broth with Fish Dumpling (*Soup*)

12/Bitter Melon with Chicken Chunks (*Fowl*)

28/Tea Melon Steamed with Pork

23/Red-Cooked Fish (*Seafood*)

魚蓉清湯
燒肉炒瓜湯
茶瓜蒸雞
魚燜豬碎肉

XI

curious	knowledgeable	adventurous
23/Bottle Gourd Melon Soup	5/Chicken Velvet and Sweet Corn Soup	21/Ridged Melon Soup with Straw Mushrooms and Bean Curd
23/Almonds with Diced Chicken (Fowl)	3/Lemon Squab (Fowl)	10/Fresh Fish and Chicken Morsels (Fowl)
3/Tomatoes with Pork	21/Black Bean Sauce with Spareribs (Pork)	13/Cellophane Noodles with Pork
47/Crab Meat with Mushrooms (Seafood)	22/Lotus Root with Beef	13/Nest of Shrimp (Seafood)

XII

curious

18/Green Pea and Diced Chicken Soup

2a/Pork Cake and Chinese Ham

12/Sweet and Sour Shrimp (Seafood)

4/Sautéed Mixed Vegetables

炒什樹火青
牛酸腿豆
李辣肉鷄
球餅粧湯

knowledgeable

9/Ham and Mustard Green Soup

22/Walnuts with Diced Chicken (Fowl)

7/Ketchup Shrimp (Seafood)

24/Braised Beef

鹹芥合火
肉汁桃腿
汁蝦鷄芥
腍丁菜
湯

adventurous

16/Clear-Simmered Mushrooms (Soup)

38/Golden Flower Jade Tree Chicken (Fowl)

9/Soured Bamboo Shoots Steamed with Beef

28/Tomatoes with Pan-Fried Fish (Seafood)

茄金清
子花蒸
煮玉北
魚樹菇
肉鷄

XIII

curious

4/Bean Curd Soup

29/Asparagus with Sliced Chicken (*Fowl*)

16/Green Beans with Roast Pork

32/Sweet and Sour Fish Bits (*Seafood*)

knowledgeable

20/Sliced Fresh Pork and Mustard Green Soup

16/Sausage Steamed with Chicken (*Fowl*)

17/Cellophane Noodles and Shrimp (*Seafood*)

26/Green Peas with Chopped Beef

adventurous

23/Bottle Gourd Melon Soup

46/Three-Ingredient Roast Duck (*Fowl*)

12/Pickled Mustard Green with Pork

14/Curry Shrimp (*Seafood*)

XIV

curious

15/Tomato Egg-Flower Soup

25/Snow Peas with Sliced Chicken (*Fowl*)

11/Bean Curd with Pork

16/Almonds with Diced Shrimp (*Seafood*)

番茄蛋花湯

雪豆雞片

肉豆腐

杏仁蝦仁雞丁

knowledgeable

11/Watercress Soup

6/Chinese Ham Steamed with Fresh Pork Slices

42/Lemon Chicken Wings (*Fowl*)

33/Choy Sum with Fish Bits (*Seafood*)

西洋菜湯

火腿蒸肉

心汁雞翼

菜心魚肉球

adventurous

17/Sea Cucumber and Abalone Soup

2/Soy Sauce Squab (*Fowl*)

10/Winter Vegetable Steamed with Beef

11/Choy Sum with Shrimp (*Seafood*)

海參鮑魚湯

豉油鴿

冬菜蒸牛肉

菜心蝦球

XV

curious

6/Clear Broth with Seasonal Vegetable (Soup)

26/Ham with Sliced Chicken (Fowl)

9/Fu Jung Shrimp (Seafood)

2/Sautéed Choy Sum (Vegetables)

knowledgeable

18/Green Pea and Diced Chicken Soup

2b/Pork Cake and Chinese Sausage (Seafood)

19/Deep-Fried Shrimp Boxes (Seafood)

25/Snow Peas with Sliced Chicken (Fowl)

adventurous

11/Watercress Soup

33/Young Ginger with Sliced Chicken (Fowl)

29/Red-Cooked Spareribs (Pork)

24/White-Water Fish (Seafood)

FOR SIX PEOPLE

curious

5/Chicken Velvet and Sweet Corn Soup

46/Three-Ingredient Roast Duck (*Fowl*)

17/Bean Sprouts with *Beef*

18/Diced Roast *Pork*

33/Choy Sum with Fish Bits (*Seafood*)

12/Sweet and Sour Shrimp (*Seafood*)

knowledgeable

21/Ridged Melon *Soup* with Straw Mushrooms and Bean Curd

30/Soy Sauce Chicken (*Fowl*)

15/Curry Beef

33/Bean Sprouts with *Pork* Tripe

54/Batter-Dipped Frogs' Legs (*Seafood*)

1/Sautéed Fresh Lobster (*Seafood*)

adventurous

12/Hair Melon *Soup*

48/Arhat Duck (*Fowl*)

35/White Cut Chicken (*Fowl*)

28/Tea Melon Steamed with *Pork*

53/Sautéed Dried Squid (*Seafood*)

49/Sautéed Rock Snails (*Seafood*)

curious	knowledgeable	adventurous
18/Green Pea and Diced Chicken *Soup*	10/Black Mushroom and Abalone *Soup*	16/Clear-Simmered Mushrooms (*Soup*)
1/Crisp Fried Squab (*Fowl*)	19/Tomatoes with Chicken (*Fowl*)	38/Golden Flower Jade Tree Chicken (*Fowl*)
23/Sweet and Sour Pork	2/Chinese Broccoli with *Beef*	25/Canton Preserved Vegetable with *Beef*
28/Tomatoes with Pan-Fried Fish (*Seafood*)	42/Oyster Sauce with Sautéed Clams (*Seafood*)	6/Arhat's Feast (*Vegetables*)
9/*Fu Jung* Shrimp (*Seafood*)	29/Dried Bean Curd with Pan-Fried Fish (*Seafood*)	37/Shredded Pork with Steamed Flatfish (*Seafood*)
25/Snow Peas with Sliced Chicken (*Fowl*)	13/Cellophane Noodles with Pork	14/Curry Shrimp (*Seafood*)

Sample Cantonese Dinners

curious	knowledgeable	adventurous
13/Fish Slices and Lettuce in Clear Broth (*Soup*)	4/Bean Curd *Soup*	3/Sliced Chicken with Shark's Fin *Soup*
11/*Choy Sum* with Chicken Morsels (*Fowl*)	26/Ham with Sliced Chicken (*Fowl*)	52/Roast Duck (*Fowl*)
13/Bean Curd with *Beef*	16/Tomatoes and Sweet Peppers with *Beef*	18/Ginger with *Beef*
1/Green Beans with *Pork*	3/Sautéed Mustard Greens (*Vegetables*)	7/Winter Vegetable Steamed with Sliced *Pork*
17/Cellophane Noodles and Shrimp (*Seafood*)	23/Sweet and Sour *Pork*	46/Sautéed Crab with Crab Roe (*Seafood*)
4/Sautéed Mixed *Vegetables*	48/Deep Fried Fresh Crab Claws (*Seafood*)	4/Sautéed Mixed *Vegetables*

IV

curious	knowledgeable	adventurous
20/Sliced Fresh Pork and Mustard Green Soup	7/Clear Broth with Fish Dumpling (Soup)	19/Winter Melon Cup (Soup)
36/Fresh Mushrooms and Chicken (Fowl)	53/Chinese Mushrooms with Duck (Fowl)	51/Cold Platter with Roast Duck (Fowl)
10/Bean Sprouts with Pork	20/Sweet and Sour Spareribs (Pork)	19/Bitter Melon with Pork
19/Deep-Fried Shrimp Boxes (Seafood)	4/Cold Sliced Bean Curd	6/Pickled Ginger with Preserved Eggs
16/Tomatoes and Sweet Peppers with Beef	33/Choy Sum with Fish Bits (Seafood)	55/King Crab with Sautéed Shredded Shark's Fin (Seafood)
2/Flaked Fish with Stirred Eggs	17/Bean Sprouts with Beef	26/Five-Stripe Fish (Seafood)

芥菜鮮肉湯

鮮菇雞片

银芽炒肉絲

炸蝦盒

茄汁牛肉

芙蓉魚片

清水魚丸湯

冬菇鴨湯

糖醋排骨

凉拌豆腐

魚心菜魚球

银芽牛肉

冬瓜盅

燒鴨拼盤

苦瓜炒肉

皮蛋子薑

蟹肉燴魚翅

五柳魚

curious	knowledgeable	adventurous
6/Clear Broth with Seasonal Vegetable (Soup)	20/Sliced Fresh Pork and Mustard Green Soup	11/Watercress Soup
41/Deep-Fried Chicken Wings (Fowl)	18/Oyster Sauce with Chicken (Fowl)	10/Fresh Fish and Chicken Morsels (Fowl)
11/Snow Peas with Beef	21/Young Ginger with Beef	13/Cellophane Noodles with Pork
34/Asparagus with Pork	3/Chinese Ham with Stirred Eggs	10/Stuffed Bitter Melon (Vegetables)
18/Green Peas with Shrimp (Seafood)	36/Steamed Butterfish (Seafood)	22/Bean Curd Pan-Fried with Fish (Seafood)
32/Sweet and Sour Fish Bits (Seafood)	36/Little Fry (Pork)	21/Top Shell with Chicken (Seafood)

VI | curious

9/Ham and Mustard Green *Soup*

13/Lobster and Chicken Chunks (*Fowl*)

4/Oyster Sauce with *Beef*

16/Green Beans with Roast *Pork*

16/Almonds and Diced Shrimp (*Seafood*)

3/Red-Cooked Bean Curd

knowledgeable

13/Fish Slices and Lettuce in Clear Broth (*Soup*)

2/Soy Sauce Squab (*Fowl*)

3/Pickled Mustard Green with *Beef*

32/Lotus Root with *Pork*

1/Chinese Sausage with Potted Rice

45/Batter-Dipped Oysters (*Seafood*)

adventurous

10/Black Mushroom and Abalone Soup

12/Bitter Melon with Chicken Chunks (*Fowl*)

15/Curry *Beef*

25/*Choy Sum* with *Pork* Tripe

29/Dried Bean Curd with Pan-Fried Fish (*Seafood*)

19/Deep-Fried Shrimp Boxes (*Sea-food*)

VII

curious

18/Green Pea and Diced Chicken Soup

50/Heart of Choy Sum with Duck (Fowl)

2a/Pork Cake with Chinese Ham

10/Bean Curd with Shrimp (Seafood)

23/Asparagus with Beef

36/Fresh Mushrooms and Chicken (Fowl)

knowledgeable

22/Sour and Hot Soup

46/Three-Ingredient Roast Duck (Fowl)

8/Mushrooms with Beef Cubes

30/Choy Sum with Sausage (Pork)

23/Red-Cooked Fish (Seafood)

18/Green Peas with Shrimp (Seafood)

adventurous

21/Ridged Melon Soup with Straw Mushrooms and Bean Curd

8/Young Ginger with Squab (Fowl)

27/Five-Spice Beef Stew

2e/Pork Cake and Salted Egg

7/Fermented Bean Curd with String beans (Vegetables)

24/White-Water Fish (Seafood)

VIII

curious

15/Tomato Egg-Flower Soup

6/Sautéed Squab in Bite-Size Pieces (*Fowl*)

19/Bean Thread with *Beef*

14/Choy Sum with Roast Pork

18/Green Peas with Shrimp (*Seafood*)

40/Deep-Fried Fresh Oysters (*Seafood*)

knowledgeable

6/Clear Broth with Seasonal Vegetable (*Soup*)

52/Roast Duck (*Fowl*)

6/Ham Steamed with *Beef*

3/Red-Cooked Bean Curd

19/Deep-Fried Shrimp Boxes (*Seafood*)

39/Chicken Livers with Sliced Chicken (*Fowl*)

adventurous

14/Pickled Mustard Green and Bean Curd Soup

40/Deep-Fried Chicken Giblets (*Fowl*)

10/Winter Vegetable Steamed with *Beef*

12/Chicken Fat Braised Black Mushrooms (*Vegetables*)

7/Ketchup Shrimp (*Seafood*)

23/Red-Cooked Fish (*Seafood*)

IX

curious

12/Hair Melon Soup

47/Sautéed Shredded Roast Duck (*Fowl*)

16/Tomatoes and Sweet Peppers with Beef

6/Chinese Ham Steamed with Fresh Pork Slices

22/Walnuts with Diced Chicken (*Fowl*)

9/Fu Jung Shrimp (*Seafood*)

knowledgeable

16/Clear-Simmered Mushrooms (*Soup*)

42/Lemon Chicken Wings (*Fowl*)

22/Lotus Root with Beef

3/Tomatoes with Pork

13/Nest of Shrimp (*Seafood*)

1/Sautéed Chinese Broccoli (*Vegetables*)

adventurous

9/Ham and Mustard Green Soup

3/Lemon Squab (*Fowl*)

14/Bitter Melon with Beef

35/Sautéed Pork Kidney

2/Deep-Fried Bean Curd

59/Red-Cooked Sea Cucumber (*Seafood*)

X curious

13/Fish Slices and Lettuce in Clear Broth (Soup)

50/Heart of Choy Sum with Duck (Fowl)

1/Sautéed Beef Cubes

29/Red-Cooked Spareribs (Pork)

4/Chicken Morsels with Potted Rice

12/Sweet and Sour Shrimp (Seafood)

knowledgeable

15/Tomato Egg-Flower Soup

13/Lobster and Chicken Chunks (Fowl)

2b/Pork Cake and Chinese Sausage

12/Chicken Fat Braised Black Mushrooms (Vegetables)

3/Pickled Mustard Green with Beef

2/Flaked Fish with Stirred Eggs

adventurous

2/Chicken Velvet and Bird's Nest Soup

45/Golden Needle Chicken Wings (Fowl)

2/Chinese Broccoli with Beef

5/Canton Preserved Vegetable Steamed with Pork

20/Sautéed Sliced Top Shell (Seafood)

2/Deep-Fried Bean Curd

XI

curious

5/Chicken Velvet and Sweet Corn Soup

23/Almonds with Diced Chicken (*Fowl*)

7/*Choy Sum* with *Beef*

4/Green Peas with Chopped *Pork*

32/Sweet and Sour Fish Bits (*Seafood*)

17/Cellophane Noodles and Shrimp (*Seafood*)

knowledgeable

11/*Watercress Soup*

43/Ketchup Chicken Wings (*Fowl*)

1/*Sautéed Beef Cubes*

10/Bean Sprouts with *Pork*

45/*Batter-Dipped Oysters* (*Seafood*)

3/*Red-Cooked Bean Curd*

adventurous

23/Bottle Gourd Melon *Soup*

55/Sweet and Sour Duck Feet (*Fowl*)

33/Young Ginger with Sliced Chicken (*Fowl*)

19/Bitter Melon with *Pork*

57/*Sautéed Eight-Ingredient Seafood Dish*

31/Chicken Fat with Carp (*Seafood*)

XII

curious

6/Clear Broth with Seasonal Vegetable (Soup)

44/Oyster Sauce Chicken Wings (Fowl)

26/Green Peas with Chopped Beef

8/Choy Sum with Pork

47/Crab Meat with Mushrooms (Seafood)

3/Chinese Ham with Stirred Eggs

knowledgeable

12/Hair Melon Soup

53/Chinese Mushrooms with Duck (Fowl)

15/Chinese Broccoli with Roast Pork

1/Fresh Shrimp with Stirred Eggs

30/Sautéed Fish Slices (Seafood)

4/Oyster Sauce with Beef

adventurous

17/Sea Cucumber and Abalone Soup

32/Curry Chicken (Fowl)

9/Soured Bamboo Shoots Steamed with Beef

5/Stuffed Bean Curd

44/Black Bean Sauce and Sautéed Clams (Seafood)

2/Sautéed Choy Sum (Vegetables)

XIII

curious

4/Bean Curd *Soup*

29/Asparagus and Sliced Chicken (*Fowl*)

8/Mushrooms with *Beef* Cubes

17/Snow Peas with Roast *Pork*

27/Sweet and Sour Fish (*Seafood*)

16/Almonds with Diced Shrimp (*Seafood*)

knowledgeable

14/Pickled Mustard Green and Bean Curd *Soup*

39/Chicken Livers with Sliced Chicken (*Fowl*)

5/Preserved Kohlrabi Steamed with *Beef*

11/Oyster Sauce with Broccoli Heart (*Vegetables*)

6/Dry-Prepared Shrimp (*Seafood*)

13/Cellophane Noodles with *Pork*

adventurous

7/Clear Broth with Fish Dumplings (*Soup*)

31/Fresh Ginger Root with Braised Chicken (*Fowl*)

31/Chinese Potato with Sausage (*Pork*)

5/Squab with *Potted Rice*

9/Fermented Bean Curd with Watercress (*Vegetables*)

40/Deep-Fried Fresh Oysters (*Seafood*)

adventurous

4/Bean Curd Soup

54/West Lake Duck (*Fowl*)

5/Preserved Kohlrabi Steamed with Beef

2/Flaked Fish with Stirred Eggs

41/Red-Cooked Crab (*Seafood*)

5/Choy Sum with Sliced Abalone (*Seafood*)

knowledgeable

1/Chicken Velvet and Shark's Fin Soup

53/Chinese Mushrooms with Duck (*Fowl*)

12/Pickled Mustard Green with Pork

56/Sautéed Three-Ingredient Seafood Dish

11/Snow Peas with Beef

42/Oyster Sauce with Sautéed Clams (*Seafood*)

XIV **curious**

15/Tomato Egg-Flower Soup

52/Roast Duck (*Fowl*)

12/Yünnan Ham with Steamed Beef

1/Oyster Sauce with Bean Curd

15/Choy Sum with Sliced Shrimp (*Seafood*)

4/Sautéed Mixed Vegetables

XV

curious

23/Bottle Gourd Melon Soup

25/Snow Peas with Sliced Chicken (Fowl)

23/Asparagus with Beef

4/Roast Pork with Stirred Eggs

43/Sweet and Sour Sautéed Clams (Seafood)

28/Tomatoes with Pan-Fried Fish (Seafood)

knowledgeable

9/Ham and Mustard Green Soup

34/Lotus Root and Sliced Chicken (Fowl)

36/Little Fry (Pork)

26/Five-Stripe Fish (Seafood)

8/Black Bean Sauce with Shrimp (Seafood)

17/Bean Sprouts with Beef

adventurous

8/Seaweed Soup

14/Steamed Salt Chicken (Fowl)

24/Braised Beef

32/Lotus Root with Pork

11/Choy Sum with Shrimp (Seafood)

36/Steamed Butterfish (Seafood)

6

THE SZECHWAN MENU

The menu presented here is typical of Szechwan restaurants in the New York area and broadly representative of Szechwan restaurants in other locales as well. Although much care has been exercised in describing the dishes, the reader should expect a certain degree of variation from restaurant to restaurant and from chef to chef. Not all the dishes listed here have their origins in Szechwan province. Moo Shu Pork (Pork, No. 1) is a specialty of Yangchow, a city near Shanghai; and many dishes prepared with brown bean paste originated in Peking. Nonetheless, Szechwan restaurants include them among other dishes that are truly Szechwanese, such as those prepared with "fish flavor." Such eclecticism is fortunate for us, since it broadens our gustatory horizons.

While the characters shown in the menu have been written according to Chinese practice (that is, vertically from top to bottom), they are frequently written in horizontal left-to-right manner on the menus of Szechwan restaurants. Phonetics appearing beside the characters approximate the sounds of Mandarin, a form of which is spoken in Szechwan. A pronunciation guide is found in the Appendix. Although the tonal system of Mandarin is less complex than that of Cantonese, the reader is not likely to be understood if he orders in Chinese. Use the guide in the intended way, by pointing to the characters.

APPETIZERS

開	胃	菜
k'ai	wei	ts'ai

Note: All entries marked with an asterisk (*) are peppery-hot.

1. HACKED CHICKEN*

Literally "cudgel chicken"; the sound of the repeated character—*pang pang*—imitates the sound of chopping. Chicken is steamed, cut into strips, then tossed with a sauce made of soy, garlic, sesame oil, sesame paste, ginger root, and plenty of Szechwan pepper and red-hot oil. It is served as a cold appetizer, but it can be extremely hot to the taste. The sesame paste gives the sauce a flavor and texture similar to those of peanut butter.

pang

pang

chi

2. MARVELOUS TASTE CHICKEN*

The literal translation of the characters is "strange-taste chicken." The name refers to an unusual sauce of garlic, honey, soy sauce, ginger root, and Szechwan pepper, which is poured over plain boiled and deboned chicken. Served cold, it is especially appropriate for summer days, but its slightly sweet, pungent flavor is delicious any time.

kuai

wei

chi

3. DRUNK CHICKEN

A whole chicken is white-water cooked (see Chapter 2: Cooking Methods, No. 12), with ginger and scallions, then cut up, salted, and marinated in whiskey or sherry for one to three days. Served cold and plain, this whimsically named appetizer has an interesting, offbeat flavor.

tsui

chi

4. STEAMED DUMPLINGS

Wheat-flour doilies are filled with chopped shrimp and ground pork seasoned with ginger root, scallions, soy sauce, and wine, then steamed and served with soy, *hoisin,* red-hot oil, or white vinegar.

cheng

chiao

5. BOILED DUMPLINGS

Wheat-flour doilies, stuffed with a hearty mixture of chopped pork, Chinese cabbage, soy sauce, sesame oil, and wine, are boiled in water, then served with separate dishes of soy sauce and white vinegar for dipping.

shui

chiao

水餃

6. FRIED DUMPLINGS

Bite-size mounds of chopped beef or pork seasoned with onions, soy sauce, ginger, wine, and sesame oil are wrapped in wheat-flour doilies and fried (not *deep-fried*) in a small amount of oil until crisp. This is a familiar favorite of many Westerners. Very good when dipped in a combination of soy sauce, white vinegar, and red-hot oil.

kuo

t'ieh

鍋貼

7. SHRIMP TOAST

A mixture of chopped raw shrimp, ginger root, wine, and other seasonings is spread on bread triangles, which are then deep-fried to make a simple but elegant appetizer. *T'u ssu* is merely a phonetic rendering of "toast."

hsia

t'u

ssu

蝦吐司

8. FIVE-SPICE BEEF

Beef that has been cured with five-spice essence is thinly sliced and served cold. Usually eaten as an appetizer, this also makes a nice main dish in the summer.

wu

hsiang

niu

jou

五香牛肉

9. THREE-DELICACY COMBINATION PLATTER

Although the ingredients may vary, the delicacies usually include some combination of shrimp, black mushrooms, chicken, duck, spiced beef, ham, and jellyfish. It's a lovely dish to look at as well as eat—particularly in the warm months. Jellyfish is somewhat like heavy cellophane noodles—transparent, threadlike, and slippery (see Food Notes: Bean Thread).

san

se

p'in

p'an

三色拼盤

10. ASSORTED HOT APPETIZERS

These are tantalizing tidbits of prawns, chicken, and
pork that have been dipped in batter and deep-fried.
Since they require time to prepare, they must often be
ordered an hour or so in advance.

che

p'in

熱拼

SOUP

湯
t'ang

1. SOUR AND HOT SOUP*

This is perhaps the most familiar soup in Szechwan
cuisine. The ingredients—such as tree ear mushrooms,
bamboo shoots, or bean curd—may vary from one restaurant to another, but the basic flavors are the same—
pepper makes it hot and vinegar adds tartness.

suan

la

t'ang

酸辣湯

2. BEAN CURD SOUP

A very good all-season soup, made with fresh bean
curd, pork slices, bamboo shoots, and black mushrooms
in a chicken broth. It is similar to the Cantonese version.

tou

fu

t'ang

豆腐湯

3. SZECHWAN CABBAGE AND SHREDDED PORK SOUP

Clear chicken broth is the base for this lovely soup
containing shredded fried pork and thinly sliced Szechwan cabbage—a spicy, crunchy preserved vegetable with
an unusual flavor.

cha

ts'ai

jou

ssu

t'ang

榨菜肉絲湯

4. HAM AND WINTER MELON SOUP

Not the elaborate soup served in the melon itself, but nevertheless very good. The clear broth, usually flavored with ginger root, contains thinly sliced Smithfield ham and bits of melon. A few snow peas may be added. Very delicate in flavor.

huo

t'ui

tung

kua

t'ang

火腿冬瓜湯

5. ABALONE AND SLICED CHICKEN SOUP

Szechwan restaurants seem to excel in this fine soup. Abalone and bamboo shoots are sliced almost wafer-thin and simmered in a subtly ginger-flavored chicken broth. Snow peas and black mushrooms are often added.

pao

yü

chi

p'ien

t'ang

鮑魚鷄片湯

6. SHARK'S FIN SOUP

Although the shark's fin has very little flavor by itself, it supplies a nice nubbly texture to chicken stock flavored with ginger root, leeks, minced pork or chicken, and usually a bit of sesame oil. Because it is expensive and usually must be ordered in advance, this is a soup for special occasions.

yü

ch'ih

t'ang

魚翅湯

CHICKEN AND DUCK

chi   ya

1. DEEP-FRIED EIGHT PIECES OF CHICKEN
Large pieces of chicken (bone in) are marinated in a
mixture of soy sauce, pepper, five-spice essence, sesame
oil, wine, and ginger root, then double-fried (see Chapter 2: Cooking Methods, No. 6). The crisp chicken
pieces, served with seasoned salt, have an unusual
spicy flavor.

cha

pa

k'uai

chi

2. BUTTON MUSHROOMS WITH CHICKEN SLICES
White meat of boned chicken is sautéed with snow
peas, bamboo shoots, water chestnuts, button mushrooms, and *bok choy*. The light sauce in which the
mixture is served is delicately flavored with a hint of
sherry. This dish is the well-known Moo Goo Gai Pan
found on American menus in Cantonese restaurants.

ma

ku

chi

p'ien

3. HIBISCUS CHICKEN SLICES
Called Chicken with Egg Sauce in English, this is a
delicate and unusual dish of white meat of chicken,
snow peas, water chestnuts, wine, and a bit of sesame
oil. If the dish is authentically made, only the egg
whites are used; when poached in the hot mixture, they
puff up to resemble the hibiscus flower. (See Food
Notes: *Fu Jung*.)

fu

jung

chi

p'ien

4. SNOW PEAS WITH CHICKEN SLICES
White meat of chicken is sautéed with snow peas,
bamboo shoots, and water chestnuts. The sauce,
slightly thickened with corn flour, does not contain
soy; soy sauce should not be added to this or to any
other pale-colored dish, since the delicate flavor would
easily be overpowered.

hsüeh

tou

chi

p'ien

5. YÜNNAN CHICKEN*

Chunks of chicken are sautéed with crushed red pepper, then lightly braised in brown sauce with straw mushrooms and snow peas. The flavor is very full and spicy-hot.

yün

nan

chi

ch'iu

6. BEAN SAUCE WITH DICED CHICKEN

Bamboo shoots, water chestnuts, and chicken, all diced, are sautéed, then simmered in brown bean sauce, which is slightly sweet. This may or may not be a spicy-hot dish, depending upon whether or not *hot* soybean paste has been added. Very much a favorite of Szechwan cuisine devotees.

chiang

pao

chi

ting

7. TA CHIN CHICKEN*

Named after a well-known painter of the early Ming dynasty, this dish, although hot to the taste, has an elusive aromatic flavor. Whole chili peppers are first browned, then sautéed with chunks of chicken and sweet peppers. Soy sauce and wine are added.

ta

chin

chi

8. WALNUTS WITH DICED CHICKEN

Chicken is sautéed with slices of ginger, then combined with wine, soy sauce, and deep-fried walnuts. There are Szechwan and Cantonese versions of this dish, and both are very good.

ho

t'ao

chi

ting

9. DICED CHICKEN AND SMALL SHRIMP

Both ingredients are quickly sautéed together in near-boiling oil with diced carrots and celery, then flavored with sesame oil. A mild dish—good in combination with peppery flavors.

pao

shuang

ting

10. KUNG PAO DICED CHICKEN *

Also called Diced Chicken with Hot Pepper Sauce. kung
Chicken that has been marinated in wine and soy sauce
is sautéed with shreds of charred dried red peppers pao
and further seasoned with sesame oil, wine, soy sauce,
and a touch of vinegar; no vegetables are included. chi
This is delicious but can be very hot. Avoid the peppers! (See Chapter 2: Cooking Methods, No. 18.) ting

11. VINEGAR SAUCE CHICKEN *

For this dish, frequently called Chunked Chicken with ts'u
Hot Sauce, large pieces of bamboo are sautéed together
with chicken chunks, ginger, scallions, and whole chili liu
peppers, and a light sweet-sour sauce is added. This
dish has an unusual combination of hot, sweet, and chi
sour flavors.

12. OIL-SPLASHED CHICKEN

In this dish, usually translated as Chunked Chicken yu
Showered with Ginger, wine, ginger, and soy sauce are
combined with heated oil and spooned over pieces of lin
poached chicken. A few snow peas and water chestnuts
are sometimes added. This is a fine dish for those just chi
getting acquainted with the flavor of ginger root, since
it is not too pervasive here.

13. ORANGE-PEEL CHICKEN *

Dried orange peel is sautéed with hot red peppers and ch'en
pieces of chicken. The magnificent bouquet of this
dish is truly singular and should be experienced by p'i
anyone interested in exploring Szechwan cuisine. The
hotness of the dish varies somewhat with the restau- chi
rant, but, in any case, *don't* confuse the darkened
orange peel with the red peppers.

14. YOUNG GINGER WITH DUCK *

Often called Tender Fried Duck with Chili Sauce, tzu
this lovely, mildly peppery dish consists of sliced young
ginger, pieces of lightly breaded and fried duck (bone chiang
in), and bamboo shoots. Sweet peppers and hot peppers make the "chili sauce." ya

15. GRAINED CHICKEN AND CELERY*

Chicken that has been finely chopped (minced to the size of grains) is mixed with chopped water chestnuts, shaped into balls, and sautéed with garlic, tree ears (tree fungus), snow peas, bamboo shoots, and celery. The sauce in which the ingredients are served is made very hot by the addition of crushed red chili peppers. Some restaurants prepare this dish with more sauce than others, and some use ketchup in the sauce.

hsiao
chien
tzu
chi

小煎子鷄

16. HOME-STYLE CHUNKED CHICKEN*

Large pieces of sautéed chicken (bone in) are braised with green peppers, bamboo shoots, onions, scallions, and tree ears (tree fungus). A nice hearty dish.

chia
ch'ang
tzu
chi

家常子鷄

17. BROKEN KERNEL CHICKEN*

Called Sautéed Wonderful Chicken on the menu, this is a very spicy-hot, delicious mixture of finely diced chicken (the size of kernels, hence its Chinese name), diced carrots and water chestnuts, shredded bamboo shoots, snow peas, and finely shredded hot peppers— all sautéed together and garnished with finely chopped peanuts.

sui
mi
chi

碎米鷄

18. SZECHWAN ROAST DUCK (literally "Flavor Crisp Duck")

The fowl is not roasted but rather steamed and deep-fried. Before cooking, the duck is seasoned with ginger, leeks, star anise, and Szechwan pepper. It is served with small dishes of sauce or flavored salt and lotus leaf rolls (steamed wheat-dough puffs). Pieces of the duck are dipped in the sauce and/or salt, then placed in a lotus leaf roll. The duck and roll are eaten together. Delicious, and one of the best-known dishes of the region.

hsiang
su
ya

香酥鴨

19. CAMPHOR AND TEA SMOKED DUCK

An entire duck is marinated in wine, soy sauce, and
star anise, and smoked over camphor wood, black tea,
and orange peel. It is then deep-fried and served either
hot or at room temperature. The flavor of this elegant
dish, similar to that of delicately smoked ham, is quite
singular.

chang
ch'a
ya

樟茶鴨

20. OIL-SPLASHED DUCK (*Shower-Fried Duck*)

Parboiled duck is showered with heated oil until crisp,
then cut up into small pieces. The duck is often served
with condiments, but be sure to savor its delicate, un-
adorned taste first.

yu
lin
ya

油淋鴨

21. SAUTÉED SHREDDED DUCK (*Sautéed Shredded Duck
with Chinese Celery*)

Roast duck is sautéed with sweet red and green peppers, bamboo shoots, black mushrooms, and Szechwan
cabbage. All ingredients are finely shredded. Delicate
seasonings of soy sauce, wine, and ginger give the dish
a lovely fresh taste.

ch'ao
ya
ssu

炒鴨絲

22. PEKING DUCK

The skin of Peking Duck, rather than the flesh, is considered the delicacy. After a complicated preliminary
preparation the duck is roasted until dark brown. The
skin, which has been basted with honey during roasting, is served separately from the meat. Pieces of the
skin, together with scallions, are dipped in *hoisin* sauce
or brown bean paste, folded up in Peking doilies
(包 餅 , *pao ping*; discs of unleavened wheat-
flour dough) and eaten with the fingers. Peking duck
must be ordered at least twenty-four hours in advance.

pei
ching
ya

北京鴨

PORK

猪

jou

Note: Jou means simply "meat"; when the character appears alone on the menu, it refers to pork.

1. Moo Shu Pork (literally "Wooden Whiskers Pork")
Everyone likes this sautéed mixture of pork, bean
sprouts, scallions, water chestnuts, tree ears (tree fungus), lily buds, and scrambled egg. The ingredients are
finely shredded and crunchy, hence the name "wooden
whiskers." The mixture is wrapped in steamed pancake
doilies by each person at the table. Care should be
taken not to overfill the pancake pouches, as they tear
rather easily. About five or six pancakes, which generally must be ordered separately, are enough for a single
order of Moo Shu Pork.

mu

hsü

jou

2. Scallions with Fried Sliced Pork
Pork slices marinated in garlic, wine, and soy sauce are
sautéed with scallions and seasoned with more soy
sauce, sesame oil, and a bit of brown bean paste. The
flavor is hearty without being overwhelming.

ts'ung

pao

jou

p'ien

3. Peking Sauce with Shredded Pork
Pork strips are seasoned with wine and soy, then deep-
fried, combined with Peking sauce, and served on a
bed of shredded ginger root and scallions. A tasty,
hearty dish, it is a good choice for newcomers to this
cuisine. Peking sauce, a mixture of *hoisin* sauce and
brown bean sauce, has a peanut butter–like flavor and
texture; its color, however, is somewhat darker than
that of peanut butter.

ching

chiang

jou

ssu

4. TWICE-COOKED PORK*
Also known as Double-Sauteed Sliced Pork or Szech-   hui
wan Pork, this is fresh lean pork which is first simmered, then sliced and cooked a second time with   kuo
garlic, green pepper, bean pastes both hot and sweet,
soy sauce, and dried bean curd. A deliciously full-fla-   jou
vored dish.

5. SWEET AND SOUR PORK
Pieces of fresh pork loin, lightly coated with corn-   t'ien
starch batter, are deep-fried, then combined with green
peppers and pineapple chunks. The sweet-sour sauce   suan
is made of sugar, vinegar, and ketchup. (Tomato
ketchup is a frequent addition to Szechwan sweet-sour   jou
dishes.)

6. WATER MARGIN PORK*
A fanciful name for a deliciously spicy-hot dish made   shui
of fried pork, sliced Chinese mushrooms, bamboo
shoots, mustard greens, and red chili peppers—all in   hu
brown gravy. "Water Margin" refers to the abode of a
band of Robin Hood–like characters in a Chinese novel   jou
of the Sung dynasty.

7. GREEN PEPPERS WITH SHREDDED PORK
Thin strips of pork are sautéed with sweet green and   ch'ing
red pepper slices, onions, and bamboo shoots, then
mildly flavored with soy sauce and wine.   chiao

jou

ssu

8. BEAN SAUCE WITH PORK
Slices of fresh pork, bamboo shoots, and sweet red and   chiang
green peppers are sautéed together, then braised in
brown bean sauce. This is a delicious and interesting   pao
flavor combination—a bit winey with a hint of sweetness.   jou

9. SZECHWAN CABBAGE (*Preserved Kohlrabi*) AND SHREDDED PORK

Strips of fresh pork and Szechwan cabbage are sautéed with bamboo shoots, ginger, and both sweet and hot peppers, then seasoned with soy sauce. Interestingly, the Cantonese version of preserved kohlrabi with pork is much more pungent than the Szechwan.

cha
ts'ai
jou
ssu

榨菜肉絲

10. GARLIC SAUCE WITH SHREDDED PORK* (literally "Fish Flavor with Shredded Pork")

The English translation certainly seems more appropriate than the Chinese name, since the flavoring ingredient is garlic, and definitely not fish (see Food Notes: Fish Flavor). This is a very spicy-hot dish of pork strips sautéed with bruised garlic; tree ears (tree fungus) and water chestnuts are added, as well as seasonings of ginger root, sesame oil, wine, and hot soybean paste.

yü
hsiang
jou
ssu

魚香肉絲

11. LION'S HEAD

Large, fried meatballs made of minced pork, chopped mushrooms, sherry, and soy sauce are served on a bed of boiled celery cabbage. Lion's Head derives its name from the size and shape of the meatballs and the shaggy, manelike appearance of the boiled cabbage around them. Although a famous Northern dish, it is not widely available in restaurants.

shih
tzu
t'ou

獅子頭

LAMB

yang   jou

1. SCALLIONS WITH SAUTÉED LAMB
Lamb slices, stir-fried with scallions and mushrooms, are served in a hearty but not spicy-hot sauce that is seasoned with ginger, wine, and sometimes a bit of sesame oil.

ts'ung

pao

yang

jou

蔥爆羊肉

2. SLICED LAMB WITH WHITE SAUCE
Flour-dipped lamb slices are braised with leeks and garlic, then combined with snow peas, bamboo shoots, fresh coriander, and sesame oil. The flour gives the sauce a whitish appearance, hence its name.

yan

pao

yang

jou

塩爆羊肉

3. YÜNNAN LAMB*
Slices of lamb simmered with whole fried chili peppers are served on a bed of greens, usually spinach. A marvelous lamb specialty of the region, but beware of the chili peppers! This dish is sometimes called Kung Pao Lamb (see Chapter 2: Cooking Methods, No 18).

yün

nan

yang

jou

雲南羊肉

BEEF

niu   jou

1. MUSHROOMS AND BAMBOO SHOOTS WITH BEEF

Bamboo shoots, snow peas, and sliced mushrooms (*champignons*) are sautéed with beef slices, then seasoned with soy sauce and garlic to make this mild but flavorsome dish.

shuang

tung

niu

jou

2. SNOW PEAS WITH BEEF

This dish, generally considered Cantonese, is flavored with garlic, soy sauce, ginger, wine, and oyster sauce. The Szechwan version uses much more garlic but no oyster sauce. It is a well-seasoned, hearty dish.

hsüeh

tou

niu

jou

3. SCALLIONS WITH BEEF

A full-flavored but not spicy-hot dish of beef slices quickly fried with scallions and mushrooms, then served in a light sauce seasoned with wine, ginger, and soy sauce.

ts'ung

pao

niu

jou

4. CASHEWS WITH BEEF

A popular and very pleasant dish combining stir-fried beef, wine, soy sauce, scallions, whole cashew nuts, and sometimes oyster sauce and/or brown bean sauce. The flavors and textures of the ingredients provide interesting contrasts.

yao

kuo

niu

jou

5. ORANGE PEEL WITH BEEF*

This ambrosial dish consists of beef slices dry-sautéed
with scallions, whole chili peppers, and dried orange
peel. The peppers can make it almost dangerously hot,
but the flavor is delectable.

ch'en

p'i

niu

jou

6. GREEN PEPPERS WITH SHREDDED BEEF

A good, simple preparation of thin strips of beef and
green peppers sautéed together and lightly flavored with
soy sauce.

ch'ing

chiao

niu

jou

ssu

7. BEAN SAUCE WITH SHREDDED BEEF

Finely shredded beef and bamboo shoots are braised
together with leeks and *ta t'ou ts'ai* (大 頭 菜 ;
see Food Notes: Preserved Vegetable), a form of preserved kohlrabi, then combined with slightly sweetened
brown bean sauce. Mild but flavorful.

chiang

pao

niu

jou

ssu

8. GARLIC SAUCE WITH SHREDDED BEEF* (literally "Fish
   Flavor with Shredded Beef")

This dish consists of scallions, ginger root, bruised garlic, and tree ears (tree fungus) sautéed with beef strips,
then seasoned with wine, soy sauce, sesame oil, and
hot soybean paste. Despite the name, don't look for
any fish flavor. The prominent flavors (*quite* prominent) are garlic and hot soybean paste. (See Food
Notes: Fish Flavor.)

yü

hsiang

niu

jou

ssu

9. PEKING SAUCE WITH SHREDDED BEEF

Deep-fried beef strips are combined with soy sauce, sweet soybean paste, wine, scallions, and ginger root. The flavors are definite but not overpowering.

ching

chiang

niu

jou

ssu

京醬牛肉絲

10. DRY-SAUTÉED SHREDDED BEEF* (Szechwan-Style Sautéed Shredded Beef)

This is one of the Szechwan "dry-sautéed" dishes—that is, one that is prepared with only a very small amount of oil. Beef, shredded carrots, scallions, and ginger root are sautéed together and seasoned with wine, sesame oil, shredded chili peppers, and hot soybean paste. The absence of any sauce or water in this dish accents the peppery, slightly smoky flavor.

kan

ch'ao

niu

jou

ssu

干炒牛肉絲

11. KUNG PAO SHREDDED BEEF*

Beef strips marinated in wine and soy sauce, then sautéed with charred dried red peppers, are seasoned with more soy sauce, wine, sesame oil, and vinegar. This dish can be very hot to uninitiated palates, but it is worth it. On the menu it is usually called Shredded Beef with Hot Pepper Sauce. (See Chapter 2: Cooking Methods, No. 18.)

kung

pao

niu

jou

ssu

宮保牛肉絲

12. SA CHIA BEEF*

Sa chia and sha ch'a are phonetic renderings of saté, the Indonesian method of barbecuing or grilling. Beef slices, braised in a peppery barbecue sauce and flavored with five-spice essence, are garnished with crunchy snow peas. The spiciness and hotness can vary, but the dish is always delicious.

sha

ch'a

niu

jou

沙茶牛肉

13. YÜNNAN-STYLE BEEF*

An excellent dish of beef cubes sautéed with black
Chinese mushrooms, straw mushrooms, and broccoli,
then simmered in a moderately spicy-hot sauce. The
first two characters represent the ancient name for
Yünnan, a province in southwestern China.

t'ien

shih

niu

jou

SEAFOOD

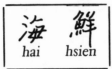

hai   hsien

1. SWEET AND SOUR FISH

Whole deep-fried fish (usually carp in Szechwan cuisine) is served with green and red sweet peppers in a
sweet-sour sauce flavored with garlic, ginger, soy sauce,
wine, and ketchup.

t'ien

suan

yü

2. RED-COOKED FISH (*Fish with Brown Sauce*)

Whole fish, usually carp, is sautéed with ginger and
scallions, then briefly braised in soy sauce and oyster
sauce. This is the Szechwan equivalent of the familiar
hung shu yü (Red-Cooked Fish) of Cantonese restaurants (Cantonese Menu: Seafood, No. 23). Although
very different from each other, both are singularly delicious.

hung

shao

yü

3. DRY-COOKED CARP* (*Carp with Hot Bean Sauce*)

Dry-cooked whole carp (no liquid added during cooking) seasoned with garlic, ginger root, wine, and soy
is covered with a rich brown sauce generously flavored
with hot soybean paste. Bamboo shoots and snow peas
are usually added to this superspicy dish. Carp is quite
bony and rather troublesome to eat, but the excellent
flavor here makes the effort most worthwhile.

kan

shao

li

yü

4. ASPARAGUS WITH ABALONE

A beautifully subtle dish of thinly sliced abalone braised in chicken broth with asparagus (usually white). The pale sauce is slightly thickened with cornstarch and flavored with wine.

lu
sun
pao
yü

露荀鮑魚

5. STRAW MUSHROOMS WITH ABALONE

A light, delicate combination of bamboo shoots, sliced abalone, ginger root, and straw mushrooms, all simmered in wine-seasoned broth.

ts'ao
ku
pao
yü

草菇鮑魚

6. SWEET AND SOUR SHRIMP

Whole shrimp, dipped in a light batter, are deep-fried, then served in sweet-sour sauce together with pineapple, lychees, and cherries. This sauce differs from that in the Cantonese version: it is sweeter, thicker, and usually red, since ketchup is often added.

t'ien
suan
hsia

甜酸蝦

7. PLAIN SAUTÉED SHRIMP

Whole shrimp are sautéed with ginger root, snow peas, and sliced bamboo shoots. Although wine and soy sauce are the only other seasonings added, the overall flavor is remarkably full-bodied.

ch'ing
ch'ao
hsia
jen

清炒蝦仁

8. CASHEWS WITH SHRIMP

Whole shrimp brushed with sesame oil are sautéed with cubed bamboo shoots, fried cashews, scallions, and ginger root. Delicate flavor and a nice crunchy texture.

yao
kuo
hsia
jen

腰菓蝦仁

9. Dry-Cooked Shrimp* (*Hot Spicy Shrimp*)
Deep-fried whole shrimp are quickly sautéed with scallions and ginger root, then combined with ketchup, hot soybean paste, and sesame oil for a rich, tangy flavor. No vegetables other than scallions are included.

kan

shao

hsia

jen

干燒蝦仁

10. Kung Pao Shrimp*
Called Sautéed Shrimp with Hot Pepper Sauce on the menu. Whole shrimp are deep-fried and served in a very spicy and peppery sauce flavored with charred shreds of dried red pepper, ginger root, garlic, wine, and soy sauce. No vegetables are included, but peanuts are often added as a garnish. (See Chapter 2: Cooking Methods, No. 18.)

kung

pao

hsia

jen

宮保蝦仁

11. Bean Curd with Shrimp
Whole shrimp marinated in ginger juice are sautéed with cubes of bean curd, leeks, and green peas, then served in a slightly thickened sauce to which a little wine is added. Although this dish is delicate in taste, its flavors are more pronounced than those of the Cantonese version.

tou

fu

hsia

jen

豆腐蝦仁

12. Crisp Fried Shrimp
Whole shrimp, marinated in sesame oil, wine, ginger, and green onion, are dipped in batter and deep-fried until golden. Especially good when served with peppered salt. No vegetables are included.

su

cha

hsia

jen

酥炸蝦仁

13. Red-Cooked Prawns (*Prawns in Brown Sauce*)
Whole or sliced prawns are braised with ginger root in soy, oyster sauce, and wine, then combined with snow peas and sliced bamboo shoots. The flavor is deep but not overpowering.

hung

shao

ming

hsia

紅燒明蝦

14. DRY-COOKED PRAWNS* (*Prawns with Chili Sauce*)
Deep-fried prawns are sautéed with garlic, ginger, scallions, chopped chili peppers, soy sauce, and wine. No vegetables are added. Can be quite hot to the taste.

kan

shao

ming

hsia

干燒明蝦

15. GARLIC SAUCE WITH SLICED PRAWNS* (literally "Fish Flavor with Sliced Prawns")
Prawns are sautéed with water chestnuts and tree ears (tree fungus), then copiously seasoned with garlic, ginger root, shredded red peppers, chopped fresh coriander, and sesame oil. In my opinion, this is one of the most delicious of the spicy-hot seafood dishes. (See Food Notes: Fish Flavor.)

yü

hsiang

hsia

p'ien

魚香蝦片

16. KETTLE-COOKED SHRIMP (*Sizzling Rice with Shrimp*)
Oven-dried boiled rice is deep-fried, then dropped into hot broth, making a hissing or sizzling sound. The rice is combined with whole shrimp, straw mushrooms, Chinese mushrooms, snow peas, bamboo shoots, and water chestnuts in a light sauce delicately flavored with ginger, wine, and sesame oil. Sizzling Rice is a special treat for the diner, since it is customarily prepared at tableside.

kuo

pa

hsia

jen

鍋巴蝦仁

17. GARLIC SAUCE WITH LOBSTER* (literally "Fish Flavor with Lobster")
Cracked lobster in shell is quickly sautéed in oil with garlic, ginger, scallions, and shredded red pepper, then braised in a bit of light soy sauce. Cloud ears (tree fungus) are usually included. Although there seem to be several variations of this dish, this one is more or less the basic one. Not all versions have the same degree of spicy-hotness, but all are delicious. (See Food Notes: Fish Flavor.)

yü

hsiang

lung

hsia

魚香龍蝦

18. DRY-COOKED LOBSTER* (*Lobster with Chili Sauce*)

Another spicy-hot "dry-cooked" dish, this one features cracked lobster in the shell that has been sautéed in a very small amount of oil together with ginger, scallions, garlic, and chopped chili peppers. Soy sauce and wine are sparingly added.

kan
shao
lung
hsia

干燒龍蝦

19. HIBISCUS CRAB MEAT

Called "Crab Meat with Egg Sauce" in English. The crab is sautéed with ginger, scallions, and snow peas, then combined with beaten egg white, which puffs up to resemble the hibiscus flower. If egg yolks are included, the "hibiscus" does not form, and though the dish is good, it is not authentic. (See Food Notes: *Fu Jung*.)

fu
jung
hsieh
jou

芙蓉蟹肉

20. SAUTÉED SLICED PRAWNS

A hint of sherry can be tasted in this fine, delicate dish of sliced bamboo shoots and snow pea pods sautéed with prawns.

ch'ao
ming
hsia
p'ien

炒明蝦片

21. SQUIRREL FISH

This dish, which is usually called Boneless Sweet and Sour Whole Fish on the menu, is made with sea bass, carp, or pike. The fish, with its backbone carefully removed, is double-fried; that is, first "oil-splashed," then deep-fried. Regally served on a large platter, the delectably crispy fish is dressed with sautéed garlic, carrots, onions, and water chestnuts, and topped with a thick sweet-sour sauce. (See Food Notes: Squirrel Fish.)

sung
shu
yü

松鼠魚

VEGETABLES

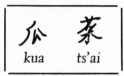

kua   ts'ai

1. STRAW MUSHROOMS WITH CABBAGE HEART

Although straw mushrooms in the United States are always canned, the flavor is still fresh and delicate. The mushrooms are braised with pieces of cabbage heart (*choy sum* in Cantonese) in a light sauce flavored with wine, ginger root, and sesame oil.

ts'ao

ku

ts'ai

hsin

2. GARLIC SAUCE WITH EGGPLANT* (literally "Fish Flavor with Eggplant")

Strips of plain eggplant are first deep-fried, then generously seasoned with ginger root, garlic, hot soybean paste, wine, and soy sauce. Delicious, but eat it sparingly at first; the flavors are very strong. (See Food Notes: Fish Flavor.)

yü

hsiang

ch'ieh

tzu

3. DRY-SAUTÉED STRING BEANS

Whole green beans are sautéed with a small amount of ground pork and dried shrimp, then flavored with soy sauce, wine, and scallions, and sometimes, depending upon the chef's whim, a bit of crushed red pepper. An excellent vegetable dish.

kan

p'ien

ssu

chi

tou

4. SAUTÉED BAMBOO SHOOTS AND BLACK MUSHROOMS

A simple but elegant dish of black Chinese mushrooms sautéed with sliced bamboo shoots, then braised in soy sauce and wine.

ch'ao

shuang

tung

5. BLACK MUSHROOMS WITH BEAN CURD

Large black mushroom caps, braised in broth with soy sauce and sesame oil, are combined with cubes of bean curd. The mushrooms are so plentiful that this dish is a veritable mycophile's delight.

tung

ku

tou

fu

6. MA PO BEAN CURD* (*Bean Curd Szechwan Style*)

This is a peppery-hot dish of ground pork sautéed with green onions, ginger root, hot soybean paste, wine, and sesame oil, and combined with bean curd. Crushed dried red pepper makes it even hotter. The *ma po* of the title literally means "pockmarked old woman"; the bean curd represents the old woman and the bits of pork the pockmarks.

ma

po

tou

fu

7. FISH FLAVOR WITH CABBAGE*

Chinese cabbage or mustard green, sautéed with very fine shreds of pork or beef, is seasoned with generous amounts of garlic and crushed dried red pepper. An unusual vegetable dish that can be very hot to the taste. (See Food Notes: Fish Flavor.)

yü

hsiang

ts'ai

t'ai

8. SAUTÉED MIXED VEGETABLES (literally "Plain Mixed Brocade")

The ingredients of this dish vary, but it usually consists of mushrooms (straw and black), bamboo shoots, scallions, tree ears (tree fungus), tiny young ears of corn, snow peas, and broccoli. Sometimes the vegetables are arranged on the platter in a pattern that indeed resembles brocade or embroidery.

su

shih

chin

9. ANTS CLIMBING TREE*

Chopped pork seasoned with onions, ginger root, soy sauce, and crushed red pepper is combined with fried or boiled bean thread (cellophane noodles). The piled-up bean thread resembles a tree and the bits of pork look like ants. Can be very hot to the taste. This dish is sometimes called Chopped Meat with Mung Bean Stick.

ma

i

shang

shu

10. MA PO STRAW MUSHROOMS* (*Mushrooms Szechwan Style*)

Straw mushrooms are combined with ground pork that has been sautéed with scallions, ginger, hot soybean paste, wine, and sesame oil. Very good spicy-hot flavor. (See No. 6 for a description of *ma po*.)

ma
po
ts'ao
ku

麻婆草菇

11. BUTTER WITH CABBAGE HEART

Variously called Cabbage Heart with Cream and Vegetable with White Sauce, this dish is unusual since both butter and milk, rarely found in Chinese cuisine, are used. Large pieces of cabbage heart (*choy sum*) or Chinese cabbage are deep-fried, then placed in a white sauce made of flour, butter, milk, and salt. It is then combined with a few straw mushrooms and baked. The sauce can vary quite a bit in thickness and quantity, depending upon the chef's style.

nai
yu
ts'ai
hsin

奶油菜心

7

ORdering from
the Szechwan menu

Typically, menus found in Szechwan restaurants are not as long as Cantonese menus. Many Szechwan restaurants have resorted to the unfortunate practice of padding their menus with recognizably Cantonese dishes or with pseudofare, such as Mu Shu Chicken. While there is nothing intrinsically wrong in ordering these dishes, it does defeat the purpose of this book, which is to offer guideposts of authenticity.

Generally speaking, Szechwan restaurants seem to be more expensive than Cantonese restaurants. Although the Szechwan portions are somewhat larger and the dishes contain more meat, I cannot definitely say that these factors account for the difference. Nevertheless, the cost of a meal in a good Szechwan restaurant is still modest by comparison with meals of comparable quality available in restaurants offering other cuisines.

The following suggestions are given to help the reader in ordering from the Szechwan menu:

1. Soup is not necessarily a part of every dinner in this cuisine, particularly during the summer.
2. If soup is not ordered, then one of the appetizers is a good choice.
3. Order one dish per person plus soup or appetizer, unless the dining party is larger than five or six persons. In that case, two appetizers are usually preferable to an additional main course.
4. Try to achieve a good balance between hot-spicy dishes and the blander ones.
5. Don't order two dishes with the same flavor, such as bean sauce with pork and bean sauce with beef.
6. Select dishes that offer a variation in the size of food pieces. If one dish is made with rather finely diced ingredients, choose others in which the ingredients are in chunks or slices.
7. A few dishes are found on both Cantonese and Szechwan menus; do not expect the tastes to be the same, since the methods of preparation can be quite different.

8

SAMPLE SZECHWAN dINNERS

Sample dinners for Szechwan cuisine to accommodate two, three or four, and six people are offered in the following pages. There are three groupings to suit different tastes and levels of sophistication—Curious, Knowledgeable, and Adventurous. The Chinese characters that appear on a Szechwan menu are sometimes written horizontally from left to right, and sometimes vertically from right to left. An asterick (*) means that the dish is peppery-hot.

Select the dinner that suits the appetite and size of your party. If some of the dishes are not available, ask for recommendations or for one of the house specialties for which Szechwan restaurants are known, or consult this guide's Szechwan Menu.

To find a description of the dishes given in the sample dinners, note the section (italics) and number (Arabic numerals) of the selections as they appear in the Szechwan Menu. For example, "(21) Sautéed Shredded Duck (*Fowl*)" is item No. 21 in the Fowl section of the Szechwan Menu.

FOR TWO PEOPLE

curious	knowledgeable	adventurous
1/Deep-Fried Eight Pieces of Chicken	3/Scallions with Beef	1/Scallions with Sautéed *Lamb*
4/Sautéed Bamboo Shoots and Black Mushrooms (*Vegetables*)	16/Kettle-Cooked Shrimp (*Seafood*)	3/Dry-Cooked Carp* (*Seafood*)

炒 八 塊 雞
雙 烘 冬 筍

鍋 巴 蝦 仁
燒 牛 肉

干 燒 鯉 魚
蔥 爆 羊 肉

curious

2/Bean Curd Soup

7/Shrimp Toast (Appetizers)

6/Green Pepper with Shredded Beef

青豆蝦羹

青椒牛肉絲

蝦吐司

牛肉絲

knowledgeable

4/Ham and Winter Melon Soup

3/Drunk Chicken (Appetizers)

8/Bean Sauce with Pork

醬鮮火

爆腿

肉雞冬

丁瓜湯

adventurous

1/Sour and Hot Soup*

2/Marvelous Taste Chicken* (Appetizers)

9/Szechwan Cabbage and Shredded Pork

榨怪酸

菜味辣

肉雞湯

絲

curious

10/Assorted Hot Appetizers

2/Button Mushrooms with Chicken Slices

8/Sautéed Mixed Vegetables

素麻熱
什菇拼
錦雞片

knowledgeable

7/Shrimp Toast (Appetizers)

21/Sautéed Shredded Duck

3/Dry-Sautéed String Beans (Vegetables)

干炒蝦
扁鴨吐
四絲司
季
豆

adventurous

5/Five-Spice Beef (Appetizers)

17/Broken Kernel Chicken*

7/Fish Flavor with Cabbage* (Vegetables)

魚碎五
香米香
菜雞牛
合肉

IV curious

2/Scallions with Fried Sliced Pork

1/Mushrooms and Bamboo Shoots
    with Beef

假蔥
叉爆
冬菰
牛肉
肉片

knowledgeable

6/Bean Sauce with Diced Chicken

9/Szechwan Cabbage and Shredded
    Pork

榨肉
菜絲
肉鷄
絲丁

adventurous

11/Vinegar Sauce Chicken*

4/Twice-Cooked Pork*

回醋
鍋溜
肉鷄

V curious

8/Five-Spice Beef (Appetizers)

1/Scallions with Sautéed Lamb

五香牛肉

葱爆羊肉

knowledgeable

1/Hacked Chicken* (Appetizers)

2/Sliced Lamb with White Sauce

怪味鷄

白爆羊肉

adventurous

9/Three-Delicacy Combination Platter (Appetizers)

13/Orange-Peel Chicken*

三色拼盤

陳皮鷄

VI

curious

5/Black Mushrooms with Bean Curd (*Vegetables*)

4/Cashews with Beef

5/Sweet and Sour Pork

knowledgeable

12/Oil-Splashed Chicken

7/Bean Sauce with Shredded Beef

3/Dry-Sautéed String Beans (*Vegetables*)

adventurous

10/Assorted Hot Appetizers

10/Kung Pao Diced Chicken*

6/Green Pepper with Shredded Beef

VII

curious

7/Shrimp Toast (Appetizers)

1/Deep-Fried Eight Pieces of Chicken

1/Straw Mushrooms with Cabbage Heart (Vegetables)

蝦多士

八塊雞

草菇菜心

knowledgeable

5/Boiled Dumplings (Appetizers)

3/Hibiscus Chicken Slices

3/Peking Sauce with Shredded Pork

水餃

芙蓉雞片

京醬肉絲

adventurous

3/Drunk Chicken (Appetizers)

10/Ma Po Straw Mushrooms* (Vegetables)

16/Sautéed Sliced Prawns (Seafood)

醉雞

麻婆草菇

炒蝦片

VIII

curious

4/Steamed Dumplings (*Appetizers*)

8/Walnuts with Diced Chicken

11/Bean Curd with Shrimp (*Seafood*)

knowledgeable

10/Assorted Hot Appetizers

9/Diced *Chicken* and Small Shrimp

1/*Moo Shu Pork*

adventurous

6/Fried Dumplings (*Appetizers*)

5/*Yünnan Chicken**

9/Peking Sauce with Shredded *Beef*

FOR THREE OR FOUR PEOPLE

curious	knowledgeable	adventurous
10/Assorted Hot Appetizers	9/Three-Delicacy Combination Platter (Appetizers)	7/Shrimp Toast (Appetizers)
2/Bean Curd Soup	4/Ham and Winter Melon Soup	3/Szechwan Cabbage and Shredded Pork Soup
2/Button Mushrooms with Chicken Slices	3/Peking Sauce with Shredded Pork	13/Orange-Peel Chicken*
8/Cashews with Shrimp (Seafood)	12/Oil-Splashed Chicken	3/Dry-Sautéed String Beans (Vegetables)

curious

5/Boiled Dumplings (*Appetizers*)

4/Twice-Cooked Pork*

6/Green Pepper with Shredded Beef

6/Sweet and Sour Shrimp (*Seafood*)

甜菁回水

餃豬鍋餃

蝦牛肉

肉

絲

knowledgeable

8/Five-Spice Beef (*Appetizers*)

11/Vinegar Sauce Chicken*

9/Szechwan Cabbage and Shredded Pork

1/Sweet and Sour Fish (*Seafood*)

甜榨醋香

酸菜溜香

肉肉雞牛

魚　絲

adventurous

2/Marvelous Taste Chicken* (*Appetizers*)

4/Sautéed Bamboo Shoots and Black Mushrooms (*Vegetables*)

6/*Ma Po* Bean Curd* (*Vegetables*)

3/Peking Sauce with Shredded Pork

京麻炒怪

醬婆味

肉肉雙

絲腐冬味

菇雞

curious

8/Walnuts with Diced Chicken

3/Dry-Sautéed String Beans (Vegetables)

12/Crisp Fried Shrimp (Seafood)

1/Moo Shu Pork

木 酥 干 核
須 炸 扁 桃
肉 蝦 李 雞
仁 丁 豆

knowledgeable

1/Scallions with Sautéed Lamb

2/Garlic Sauce with Eggplant*
(Vegetables)

4/Cashews with Beef

17/Broken Kernel Chicken*

碎 煙 爆 葱
米 魚 香 爆
雞 牛 茄 羊
肉 丁 子 肉

adventurous

12/Sa Chia Beef*

10/Kung Pao Shrimp* (Seafood)

19/Camphor and Tea Smoked Duck

11/Butter with Cabbage Heart
(Vegetables)

奶 樟 宮 沙
油 茶 保 茶
菜 鴨 蝦 牛
心 仁 肉

IV curious

8/Five-Spice Beef (*Appetizers*)

9/Diced Chicken and Small Shrimp

3/Peking Sauce with Shredded *Pork*

3/Dry-Sautéed String Beans (*Vegeta-bles*)

knowledgeable

7/Shrimp Toast (*Appetizers*)

8/Walnuts with Diced Chicken

1/Moo Shu Pork

7/Bean Sauce with Shredded Beef

adventurous

1/Hacked Chicken* (*Appetizers*)

9/Szechwan Cabbage and Shredded Pork

3/Dry-Cooked Carp* (*Seafood*)

8/Sautéed Mixed Vegetables

V **curious**

12/Oil-Splashed Chicken

5/Sweet and Sour Pork

6/Green Peppers with Shredded Beef

4/Sautéed Bamboo Shoots and Black Mushrooms (Vegetables)

knowledgeable

20/Oil-Splashed Duck

1/Scallions with Sautéed Lamb

9/Peking Sauce with Shredded Beef

7/Fish Flavor with Cabbage* (Vegetables)

adventurous

15/Grained Chicken and Celery*

11/Lion's Head (Pork)

11/Kung Pao Shredded Beef*

20/Sautéed Sliced Prawns (Seafood)

VI

curious

2/Bean Curd Soup
4/Snow Peas with *Chicken Slices*
1/Sweet and Sour Fish (*Seafood*)
2/Sliced *Lamb* with White Sauce

knowledgeable

1/Sour and Hot Soup*
18/Szechwan Roast Duck
2/Red-Cooked Fish (*Seafood*)
1/Mushrooms and Bamboo Shoots with *Beef*

adventurous

3/Szechwan Cabbage and Shredded Pork Soup
10/Garlic Sauce with Shredded *Pork**
12/*Sa Chia Beef**
6/Bean Sauce with Diced *Chicken*

VII

curious	knowledgeable	adventurous
1/Deep-Fried Eight Pieces of Chicken	16/Home-Style Chunked Chicken*	2/Marvelous Taste Chicken* (Appetizers)
2/Scallions with Fried Sliced Pork	3/Peking Sauce with Shredded Pork	6/Water Margin Pork*
7/Plain Sautéed Shrimp (Seafood)	4/Asparagus with Abalone (Seafood)	5/Straw Mushroms with Abalone (Seafood)
11/Butter with Cabbage Heart (Vegetables)	3/Dry-Sautéed String Beans (Vegetables)	9/Ants Climbing Tree* (Vegetables)

炸清葱炒
油炸葱八
菜蝦燒爆
心肉塊
仁片雞

干家京宫
烯路醬保
四蓉肉鸡
季鲍子
豆片絲雞

螞客水怪
蟻蘆菇濟味
上鲍肉雞
樹魚

VIII

curious

21/Sautéed Shredded Duck

7/Green Peppers with Shredded Pork

4/Cashews with Beef

8/Sautéed Mixed Vegetables

knowledgeable

8/Bean Sauce with Pork

2/Garlic Sauce with Eggplant*
(Vegetables)

5/Black Mushrooms with Bean Curd
(Vegetables)

11/Vinegar Sauce Chicken*

adventurous

19/Camphor and Tea Smoked Duck

3/Yünnan Lamb*

4/Twice-Cooked Pork*

11/Butter with Cabbage Heart
(Vegetables)

curious	knowledgeable	adventurous
IX		
3/Hibiscus Chicken Slices	2/Sliced Lamb with White Sauce	6/Fried Dumplings (Appetizers)
1/Scallions with Sautéed Lamb	13/Yünnan-Style Beef*	21/Sautéed Shredded Duck
8/Bean Sauce with Pork	8/Cashews with Shrimp (Seafood)	17/Broken Kernel Chicken*
1/Straw Mushrooms with Cabbage Heart (Vegetables)	5/Black Mushrooms with Bean Curd (Vegetables)	8/Garlic Sauce with Shredded Beef*

X curious

4/Ham and Winter Melon Soup

10/Assorted Hot Appetizers

2/Button Mushrooms with Chicken Slices

9/Peking Sauce with Shredded Beef

京醬肉絲

火腿冬瓜湯

什錦熱葷

蘑菇鷄片

knowledgeable

6/Shark's Fin Soup

3/Drunk Chicken (Appetizers)

1/Moo Shu Pork

12/Crisp Fried Shrimp (Seafood)

鮮魚翅

醉鷄

炸須湯

鍋肉

蝦仁

adventurous

5/Abalone and Sliced Chicken Soup

9/Three-Delicacy Combination Platter (Appetizers)

13/Orange-Peel Chicken*

10/Dry-Sautéed Shredded Beef*

干煸三鮮鮑

炒皮絲

牛肉絲鷄

陳皮湯

FOR SIX PEOPLE

curious

10/Assorted Hot Appetizers
2/Button Mushrooms with Chicken Slices
3/Peking Sauce with Shredded Pork
3/Scallions with Beef
1/Sweet and Sour Fish (Seafood)
3/Dry-Sautéed String Beans (Vegetables)

knowledgeable

5/Boiled Dumplings (Appetizers)
6/Bean Sauce with Diced Chicken
1/Scallions with Sautéed Lamb
4/Twice-Cooked Pork*
12/Sa Chia Beef*
4/Asparagus with Abalone (Seafood)

adventurous

7/Shrimp Toast (Appetizers)
5/Yünnan Chicken*
10/Garlic Sauce with Shredded Pork*
9/Peking Sauce with Shredded Beef
21/Squirrel Fish (Seafood)
6/Ma Po Bean Curd* (Vegetables)

curious

8/Five-Spice Beef (Appetizers)

3/Hibiscus Chicken Slices

5/Sweet and Sour Pork

7/Bean Sauce with Shredded Beef

8/Cashews with Shrimp (Seafood)

8/Sautéed Mixed Vegetables

素燴蝦澄甜美五

什果煤酸含香

錦蝦牛肉雞牛

片肉肉熬肉

knowledgeable

3/Drunk Chicken (Appetizers)

1/Moo Shu Pork

3/Yünnan Lamb*

9/Peking Sauce with Shredded Beef

13/Red-Cooked Prawns (Seafood)

2/Garlic Sauce with Eggplant*
(Vegetables)

魚坂宮木醉

香烤燕醬雞

知咖牛肉雞

子蝦絲肉

adventurous

2/Marvelous Taste Chicken* (Appetizers)

19/Camphor and Tea Smoked Duck

6/Water Margin Pork*

11/Kung Pao Shredded Beef*

5/Straw Mushrooms with Abalone
(Seafood)

9/Ants Climbing Tree* (Vegetables)

螞芽宮水樟怪

蟻菰保牛

上鮑肉肉鴨雞

樹魚

☰

curious

2/Bean Curd Soup

8/Walnuts with Diced Chicken

8/Bean Sauce with Pork

2/Snow Peas with Beef

6/Sweet and Sour Shrimp (Seafood)

4/Sautéed Bamboo Shoots and Black Mushrooms (Vegetables)

knowledgeable

1/Sour and Hot Soup*

9/Diced Chicken and Small Shrimp

18/Szechwan Roast Duck

2/Scallions with Fried Sliced Pork

10/Dry-Sautéed Shredded Beef*

2/Red-Cooked Fish (Seafood)

adventurous

5/Abalone and Sliced Chicken Soup

10/Kung Pao Diced Chicken*

9/Szechwan Cabbage and Shredded Pork

8/Garlic Sauce with Shredded Beef*

7/Plain Sautéed Shrimp (Seafood)

7/Fish Flavor with Cabbage* (Vegetables)

IV curious

7/Shrimp Toast (*Appetizers*)

4/Snow Peas with Chicken Slices

2/Scallions with Fried Sliced Pork

4/Cashews with Beef

20/Sautéed Sliced Prawns (*Seafood*)

5/Black Mushrooms with Bean Curd (*Vegetables*)

knowledgeable

10/Assorted Hot Appetizers

21/Sautéed Shredded Duck

6/Water Margin Pork*

7/Bean Sauce with Shredded Beef

16/Kettle-Cooked Shrimp (*Seafood*)

10/Ma Po Straw Mushrooms* (*Vegetables*)

2/Sliced Lamb with White Sauce

adventurous

6/Fried Dumplings (*Appetizers*)

16/Home-Style Chunked Chicken*

13/Yünnan-Style Beef*

3/Dry-Cooked Carp* (*Seafood*)

15/Garlic Sauce with Sliced Prawns* (*Seafood*)

3/Dry-Sautéed String Beans (*Vegetables*)

V **curious**

3/Drunk Chicken (Appetizers)

1/Scallions with Sautéed Lamb

1/Mushrooms and Bamboo Shoots with Beef

12/Crisp Fried Shrimp (Seafood)

3/Peking Sauce with Shredded Pork

8/Sautéed Mixed Vegetables

knowledgeable

4/Steamed Dumplings (Appetizers)

15/Grained Chicken and Celery*

3/Peking Sauce with Shredded Pork

6/Green Peppers with Shredded Beef

2/Garlic Sauce with Eggplant* (Vegetables)

14/Dry-Cooked Prawns* (Seafood)

adventurous

1/Hacked Chicken* (Appetizers)

3/Yünnan Lamb*

11/Lion's Head (Pork)

8/Garlic Sauce with Shredded Beef*

4/Ma Po Bean Curd* (Vegetables)

16/Sautéed Sliced Prawns (Seafood)

adventurous

1/Sour and Hot Soup*
12/Oil-Splashed Chicken
3/Peking Sauce with Shredded Pork
7/Bean Sauce with Shredded Beef
9/Dry-Cooked Shrimp* (Seafood)
7/Fish Flavor with Cabbage* (Vegetables)

鱼香菜苔　酸辣汤
京醬肉絲
黃醬牛肉絲
乾燒蝦仁
油爆鸡

knowledgeable

3/Szechwan Cabbage and Shredded Pork Soup
11/Lion's Head (Pork)
11/Kung Pao Shredded Beef*
7/Plain Sautéed Shrimp (Seafood)
7/Fish Flavor with Cabbage* (Vegetables)
1/Scallions with Sautéed Lamb

榨菜肉絲湯
清燉獅子頭
宫保牛肉絲
炒蝦仁
鱼香菜苔
葱爆羊肉

curious

VI

4/Ham and Winter Melon Soup
9/Diced Chicken and Small Shrimp
7/Green Peppers with Shredded Pork
19/Hibiscus Crab Meat (Seafood)
2/Snow Peas with Beef
4/Sautéed Bamboo Shoots and Black Mushrooms (Vegetables)

火腿冬瓜湯
炒双丁
青椒肉絲
芙蓉蟹肉
雪豆牛肉
冬笋炒香菇

VII

curious

4/Steamed Dumplings (Appetizers)

21/Sautéed Shredded Duck

9/Peking Sauce with Shredded Beef

1/Straw Mushrooms with Cabbage Heart (Vegetables)

8/Cashews with Shrimp (Seafood)

2/Scallions with Fried Sliced Pork

蒸 煙 草 一 炒 茶

爆 菇 + 醬 鴨 殷

肉 蝦 菜 牛 絲

片 仁 心 絲

knowledgeable

2/Marvelous Taste Chicken* (Appetizers)

9/Szechwan Cabbage and Shredded Pork

4/Cashews with Beef

19/Hibiscus Crab Meat (Seafood)

3/Yünnan Lamb*

3/Dry-Sautéed String Beans (Vegetables)

干 怪 芙 腰 榨 怪

扁 南 蓉 果 菜 味

四 学 蟹 牛 肉 雞

豆 肉 肉 肉 絲

adventurous

9/Three-Delicacy Combination Platter (Appetizers)

13/Orange-Peel Chicken*

12/Sa Chia Beef*

10/Kung Pao Shrimp* (Seafood)

2/Garlic Sauce with Eggplant* (Vegetables)

4/Sautéed Bamboo Shoots and Mushrooms (Vegetables)

炒 燴 宮 沙 陳 三

雙 爆 保 茶 皮 色

冬 加 蝦 牛 雞 拼

子 仁 肉 鷄 盤

VIII

curious

9/Three-Delicacy Combination Platter (Appetizers)

1/Moo Shu Pork

6/Green Peppers with Shredded Beef

8/Cashews with Shrimp (Seafood)

5/Black Mushrooms with Bean Curd (Vegetables)

3/Dry-Sautéed String Beans (Vegetables)

干煸腰青木三
四炒菇果椒須
季豆蝦牛肉拼
豆腐仁絲盘

knowledgeable

1/Hacked Chicken* (Appetizers)

2/Sliced Lamb with White Sauce

8/Bean Sauce with Pork

15/Garlic Sauce with Sliced Prawns* (Seafood)

2/Snow Peas with Beef

4/Sautéed Bamboo Shoots and Black Mushrooms (Vegetables)

炒鲜雪醬葱棒
雙豆爆爆棒棒
冬牛蝦肉羊雞
菇片肉

adventurous

4/Steamed Dumplings (Appetizers)

14/Young Ginger with Duck*

4/Twice-Cooked Pork*

5/Orange Peel with Beef*

19/Hibiscus Crab Meat (Seafood)

8/Sautéed Mixed Vegetables

素美陳回子蒸
什蓉皮鍋姜餃
錦蟹牛肉鴨
肉肉

IX | curious

4/Ham and Winter Melon Soup

18/Szechwan Roast Duck

5/Sweet and Sour Pork

7/Plain Sautéed Shrimp (Seafood)

1/Straw Mushrooms with Cabbage Heart (Vegetables)

3/Scallions with Beef

火腿冬瓜湯
四川燒鴨
甜酸豬肉
清炒蝦仁
草菇菜心
蔥爆牛肉

knowledgeable

6/Shark's Fin Soup

12/Oil-Splashed Chicken

7/Green Peppers with Shredded Pork

13/Yunnan-Style Beef*

3/Dry-Cooked Carp* (Seafood)

3/Dry-Sautéed String Beans (Vegetables)

魚翅湯
淋油燒雞
青椒肉絲
雲南牛肉
乾燒鯉魚
乾扁四季豆

adventurous

3/Szechwan Cabbage and Shredded Pork Soup

17/Broken Kernel Chicken*

8/Bean Sauce with Pork

10/Dry-Sautéed Shredded Beef*

11/Butter with Cabbage Heart (Vegetables)

15/Garlic Sauce with Sliced Prawns* (Seafood)

榨菜肉絲湯
碎米雞
醬爆肉
乾煸牛肉絲
奶油菜心
魚香蝦片

X | **curious**

1/Deep-Fried Eight Pieces of Chicken

2/Sliced *Lamb* with White Sauce

7/Green Peppers with Shredded *Pork*

4/Sautéed Bamboo Shoots and Black Mushrooms (*Vegetables*)

9/Peking Sauce with Shredded *Beef*

11/Bean Curd with Shrimp (*Seafood*)

knowledgeable

20/Oil-Splashed *Duck*

10/Garlic Sauce with Shredded *Pork**

7/Bean Sauce with Shredded *Beef*

6/*Ma Po Bean Curd** (*Vegetables*)

16/Kettle-Cooked Shrimp (*Seafood*)

8/Sautéed Mixed Vegetables

adventurous

11/*Vinegar Sauce Chicken**

22/*Peking Duck* (advance order)

9/Szechwan Cabbage and Shredded Pork

3/*Scallions with Beef*

14/*Dry-Cooked Prawns** (*Seafood*)

7/Fish Flavor with Cabbage* (*Vegetables*)

9

food NOTES

This glossary identifies in both Cantonese and Mandarin phonetics the various ingredients mentioned in this book. In some instances, completely different written forms are used in the two dialects; and occasionally so many different characters exist for a single item that a complete listing would be folly. What I have attempted in such cases is to use the written forms that will be most generally understood, should the reader have reason to show them to a restaurant waiter. When either Cantonese or Mandarin is given alone, that particular foodstuff or flavoring is used only by the group that speaks that dialect. Phonetic guides for Cantonese and Mandarin can be found on pages 225 and 228, respectively.

Origins and usage of certain foods are often so hazy that even the most assiduous research can lead to dead ends. In circumstances such as these I have presented the available information and, when conjecture seemed unavoidable, have indicated as much.

— 186 —

Pronunciation Key: Cantonese/Mandarin

ABALONE 鮑魚 bau yü/pao yü

Abalone is a large rock-clinging mollusk (genus *Haliotis*) having a flattened, slightly spiral shell with a nacreous lining. Its firm, resilient flesh is valued by the Chinese as an ingredient for various dishes. Except in restaurants along the West Coast, where it is one of the native fauna, abalone is not available fresh; it is either dried or canned. Don't let this keep you from trying it, however; it's very good.

AGAR-AGAR 東洋菜 tung yang choy/tung yang ts'ai

Several red algae of the genera *Gelidium* and *Gracilaria* (in particular, *Gracilaria lichenoides*) are the source of a gelatinous carbohydrate known as agar-agar, a name of Malay origin meaning jelly. Used by the Chinese as a stabilizing agent in much the same way as Americans use unflavored gelatin, agar-agar is often called Chinese gelatin. The resemblance to true gelatin, however, is mostly physical, since the latter, being animal-derived, has a high protein content, whereas the algal variety is primarily carbohydrate. Agar-agar, in the form of thin transparent strands (*ito kanten* in Japanese), is used in salads and cold dishes. In this form, it looks somewhat like bean thread (cellophane noodles).

ALMOND 杏仁 hang yan/hsing jen

Although almonds have long been known in China and are widely used in savory as well as sweet dishes, they are not native to that country, but rather to the countries of southwestern Asia. Interestingly, the characters for almond literally mean "apricot kernel." Almonds and apricots are in fact closely related (genus *Prunus*). Apricots originated in China, and the Chinese may have long been familiar with some of the apricot varieties whose kernels are edible. This may account for the Chinese name "apricot kernel."

ANCIENT EGGS. See Eggs: *Preserved Eggs.*

ARHAT'S FEAST 羅漢齋 *lo han chai* (Cantonese)

The Hinayana sect of Buddhism describes an ideal being, the Arhat (*Lo Han* in Chinese), who freed himself from worldly conflict, thus attaining the final beatitude of nirvana.

Arhat's Feast, also known as Monk's Food or Buddha's Delight, is thus called because it is vegetarian, in accordance with Buddhist dietary principles, and contains more than enough ingredients to be called a feast. Black mushrooms, tree fungi, celery cabbage, gingko nuts, bean thread, dried bean curd, and fermented bean curd are some of the usual ingredients, but others may be substituted or added in accord with the chef's imagination.

ARROWHEAD 茨菇 see *gu/tz'u ku*

An aquatic plant of the genus *Sagittaria*, whose fleshy tubers are used as food by the Chinese; certain species of these plants were also eaten by the American Indians. In some areas of California, Chinese farmers now cultivate this tuber. In its fresh state the arrowhead tuber looks like a fresh-water chestnut; when its is cooked its texture is quite mealy, very much like that of a potato (another name for it is "tule potato"). Its delicate flavor, with an occasional trace of sweetness, is an excellent complement to the rich-tasting Chinese sausage with which it is often served.

ASPARAGUS 露荀 *lei sun* (Cantonese); 龍鬚菜 *lung hsü ts'ai* (Mandarin)

The Cantonese-speaking people call asparagus "dew shoots," whereas the Mandarin-speaking people refer to it as "dragon's beard vegetable." The reason for this difference is at least partially due to the fact that asparagus is not known in China itself, even though it is adapted to Chinese cuisine here.

BAMBOO SHOOTS 竹笋 *juk sun/chu sun*

Bamboo is a versatile plant belonging to genera of grasses, chiefly tropical. The tender, young, edible shoots are harvested at least three times a year. Most bamboo shoots served in restaurants here are canned in the Far East, and are of the winter harvest. Therefore one may see "winter bamboo" in a recipe or on a menu. If any small white granules are found while eating or preparing bamboo shoots, just brush them off; they are merely calcium deposits that have formed within the plant sprout. Fresh bamboo shoots are now often found in local Chinese markets.

BAMBOO SHOOTS, *Soured* 笋衣 *sun yi/sun i*

The hulls rather than the shoots themselves are preserved in vinegar and salt, making a very pungent and tasty accompaniment for pork or beef. They are usually called pickled bamboo shoots or soured bamboo in English; in Chinese the characters translate as "shoots' clothing."

BEAN CURD, *Dried* 腐竹 *fu juk/fu chu*

Dried bean curd is prepared from soybeans that have been crushed and strained to remove the hulls. The resulting liquid is boiled in large vats until a skin resembling bamboo forms at the top. This skin, called fermented bamboo in Chinese, is peeled off in large sheets and the liquid allowed to boil again. Each time the liquid reaches the boiling point, another layer of skin forms, and the peeling process is repeated.

At a certain point in the process the skin becomes darker and sweeter as a result of natural sugar concentration or the addition of slab sugar. This form of the curd is called second bamboo or sweet bamboo (二竹 *yi juk/erh chu*).

The texture of both these forms of bean curd is pleasantly firm and chewy, very much like the texture of meat. Hence dried bean curd is used as "meat" in vegetarian dishes such as Arhat's Feast (Monk's Food).

BEAN CURD, *Fresh*　豆腐　dou fu/tou fu

Soybean flour suspended in water is curdled by an enzyme action similar to that by which cheese is made from milk. The resulting high-protein product, which resembles the curd of milk or a firm, pale cream-colored custard, is then molded into 3″ x 3″ x 1″ cakes.

It is also called bean cake, bean custard, and vegetable cheese, and all of its names are descriptive of its appearance. Although bean curd hasn't much flavor in itself, it absorbs other flavors very well and adds textural interest.

BEAN CURD, *Red Preserved*　南乳　nam yü/nan ju

Sometimes called southern cheese (its characters translate as "southern milk") or red Chinese cheese, red preserved bean curd is made of pressed soybean cake, which is fermented in rice wine, spices, and salt and colored with red rice, which turns the curd a deep brick red. The taste and aroma become stronger with aging—but not as strong as the white preserved curd—and it assumes a nutlike flavor when spooned into braised dishes.

BEAN CURD, *White Preserved*　腐乳　fu yee/fu ju

Also known as white bean curd cheese and white Chinese cheese, this type of preserved bean curd is made of pressed soybean curd fermented in wine and salt. The curd, cream-colored when it is made, becomes darker and stronger in flavor the longer it stands. Some people find it similar in taste and texture to Camembert. A few of its better-known uses are with spinach and watercress and in Arhat's Feast (Monk's Food).

BEAN PASTE, *Black*. See Black Bean.

BEAN PASTE, *Brown*. See Yellow Bean.

BEAN PASTE, *Hot*. See Yellow Bean.

BEAN SAUCE, *Black*. See Black Bean.

BEAN SAUCE, *Brown*. See Yellow Bean.

BEAN SPROUTS 豆芽菜 dou nga choy/tou ya ts'ai
Two types of bean sprouts are used in Chinese cooking:
mung bean sprouts and soybean sprouts. Mung bean
sprouts are those served in most Chinese-American restaurants, whereas soybean sprouts are usually preferred by the
Chinese. Both types are quite easily grown, but mung bean
sprouts grow twice as fast as soybean sprouts—about three
days and six days respectively.

BEAN THREAD 粉絲 fen see/fen ssu
Also called cellophane noodles (*harusame* in Japanese),
bean thread is the extruded form of paste made from
mung bean starch. The "noodles" are thin, very slippery
when cooked, and transparent—hence the name "cellophane." Bean thread has very little flavor when eaten
alone but, like bean curd, it readily absorbs the flavors of
foods with which it is combined.

BEANS 豆 dou/tou
In contrast to the often arbitrary distinction in English
between peas and beans and their associated products, the
Chinese language does not differentiate between the two,
at least not in common usage. Whereas in English one
would translate the Chinese characters 雪豆 and
豆仔 as "snow peas" and "green beans" respectively,
the Chinese use the same character 豆 for both peas and
beans. Many kinds of beans and their related products are
widely used in Chinese kitchens. For the sake of brevity
their descriptions (see individual entries) are limited to
those beans and bean products that are specifically mentioned in this book, or which are important in the preparation of the dishes. These are: black, string, mung, soy,
and yellow (brown), and their associated products.

BIRD'S NEST　燕窩　*yin wo/yen wo*

The nests from which the Oriental delicacy Bird's Nest Soup is prepared are built by small birds called swiftlets. Although these birds superficially resemble swallows (the Chinese characters read "swallow's nests"), they belong to a particular genus of swifts (*Collocalia*). While members of this genus commonly have highly developed salivary glands, certain species are capable of producing saliva in such quantity that their nests are built almost entirely of this agglutinative material. The birds reinforce the shelters with a certain red alga, *Gracilaria spinosa*. These are the nests that are so highly esteemed by the Chinese.

The nests, which take more than a month to build, are found in limestone caverns along the coast of Indochina. "Harvesters" gather them by knocking them off the cave walls with long poles. Because of the difficulty in obtaining the nests, and the subsequent painstaking labor involved in separating feathers from the edible portions, they are one of the most expensive items to be found in Oriental markets. Swiftlet nests are reputed to have a high protein content, which, if true, may derive from salival enzymes—enzymes themselves being proteins. Packaged nests in groceries look much like coconut.

BLACK BEAN

A small, black variety of soybean, the base of black bean paste and black bean sauce. The paste (豆豉 *dou see/tou ch'ih*)is made with crushed beans that have been heavily salted, fermented, and sometimes spiced. The sauce (豆豉汁 *dou see jap/tou ch'ih chih*), commonly used in Cantonese cuisine with chicken, pork, beef, or seafood, is a mixture of the paste with scallions, garlic, and ginger. It is a distinctive, pungent flavor that has no counterpart in Western cuisines.

BOK CHOY. See Cabbage: *Chinese Cabbage.*

BROCCOLI, *Chinese* 芥蘭 *gai lan/chieh lan*

Like its Western counterpart, Chinese broccoli belongs to the mustard family, but is slightly stronger in flavor. The characters for Chinese broccoli are sometimes translated as "mustard cabbage." It should not, however, be confused with mustard green.

BROWN SAUCE

The term "brown sauce" or "brown gravy" in Chinese cooking refers to ingredients usually added to a dish near the end of the cooking period. There are two basic types of this gravy. One is made of water, stock, soy sauce, cornstarch, and optional seasonings; the other consists of soy sauce, juice drippings, and bead molasses.

CABBAGE

Regardless of the literal meanings of their characters, many vegetables used by the Chinese are translated into English as "cabbage." Although almost all these belong to the same genus, *Brassica*, which includes mustard, cauliflower, kohlrabi, and turnip as well as cabbage, the use of such a broad taxonomic term is often misleading. A few of these vegetables are defined here in greater detail.

Celery Cabbage 天津菜 *tin jeun choy/t'ien chin ts'ai*

Celery cabbage, which is no relative of celery, is similar in appearance to romaine lettuce. It has pale yellow-green leaves shaped into a long, narrow, semicompact head. This moderately sharp-flavored green is generally called "Tientsin vegetable" in Chinese, but the Cantonese use the fanciful name "dragon's tooth white" (龍牙白 *lung nga bak*) as well. Many people incorrectly refer to this vegetable as Chinese cabbage.

Chinese Cabbage 白菜 *bak choy/pai ts'ai*

This is the familiar *bok choy*, whose Chinese meaning is "white vegetable." It is also known as Shantung cabbage. Stronger in flavor than celery cabbage, it has heavy, smooth white stalks topped with large, limp, dark-green leaves. Interestingly, the seed of this cabbage was exported many decades ago from China to America, where it was cultivated into a superior variety and then reintroduced to China.

Szechwan Cabbage. See Preserved Vegetable: *Szechwan Preserved Vegetable.*

CABBAGE HEART 菜心 choy sum/ts'ai hsin

This vegetable, whose characters literally translate as "vegetable heart," is a cousin to the Chinese cabbage, *bok choy*. Cabbage heart, the familiar *choy sum* of Cantonese cuisine, is allowed to grow to maturity before being picked. The large outer leaves and stalks are then discarded, leaving the more delicate leaves and stalks of the heart itself. It is smaller than *bok choy* and not as cabagey in flavor.

CARP 鯉魚 lei yü/li yü

The carp, highly regarded in Chinese cuisine, represents vigor and endurance in Chinese literature and painting. Szechwan-style restaurants generally serve it as part of the regular fare, whereas Cantonese restaurants usually reserve it for special dishes. On Szechwan menus, the word "fish" alone typically refers to carp; on Cantonese menus, at least in New York, the single word "fish" often indicates sea bass.

CELLOPHANE NOODLES. See Bean Thread.

CHAH SHU. See Pork, *Roast.*

CHICKEN 雞 or 鷄 gai/chi

In addition to these two characters, Chinese also use the character 鳳 (fung/feng), "phoenix," for the word "chicken" when it appears in certain dishes on a menu (see Cantonese Menu: Fowl, No. 39). The use of "phoenix," a mythical bird, in the name of a dish is typical of the vocabulary of Chinese menus, which borrow freely from myth, poetry, and fancy.

CHILI SAUCE

A very spicy-hot mixture of crushed small red chili peppers, apricots, garlic, lemon, and salt. It is used both as a condiment and as a flavoring in various dishes.

CHINESE CELERY　香芹　heung kin/shiang chyn

Chinese celery is much thinner and sharper in flavor than the Western variety, and is also considerably tougher.

CHINESE RESTAURANT SYNDROME. See Monosodium Glutamate.

CHOPSTICKS　筷子　faai ji/k'uai tzu

Chopsticks have been used in China since at least the fourth century B.C. In later centuries, their use was disseminated to other Asian countries that were influenced by Chinese culture. The materials of which chopsticks are made, as well as their length and shape, vary among the countries where they are used. Chinese chopsticks are about 9½ inches long, blunt-tipped, and ordinarily made of smoothly finished bamboo. More elegant table chopsticks, formerly made of bone or ivory, are now often made of plastic. Longer bamboo chopsticks are used as cooking utensils for stir-frying or as serving sticks at large tables, where reaching for the food might be difficult. Chinese chopsticks are almost always inscribed with characters that wish the diner long life, prosperity, and happiness.

Japanese chopsticks are about 1½ inches shorter than the ordinary Chinese chopsticks. They are also thinner and have pointed tips. Many Japanese households have adopted the rather common restaurant practice of using disposable chopsticks made of plain, unfinished bamboo.

For special occasions, however, such as when guests come for dinner, most households set the table with the much more refined lacquered chopsticks.

CHOY SUM. See Cabbage Heart.

CORIANDER (Mandarin) 芫荽 yun sai (Cantonese); 香菜 hsiang ts'ai

Other names for this oddly flavored herb (*Coriandrum sativum*) include Chinese parsley, cilantro, and culantro. It is a cousin to true parsley, both being members of the carrot family (*Umbelliferae*). The coriander *fruit*, improperly called its seed, has been cultivated and used by the Chinese from the fifth century B.C. Coriander *leaf*, which has a totally different taste from the fruit, is used by the Chinese as a flavor for fish soups and other dishes mentioned in this book. It is something of a contradiction that this same plant, whose characters in Mandarin literally mean "fragrant vegetable," is also one of the bitter herbs eaten at Passover. This contradiction seems to be underscored by the numbers of people who adore the taste as well as by the numbers who cannot abide it.

CORN 粟米 syut mai (Cantonese); 玉米 yü mi (Mandarin)

Although corn is not native to China, it was introduced by the Portuguese in the sixteenth century via Fuchow, Macao, or Canton. Since World War II the use of corn in Chinese cuisine has become quite extensive, particularly in Szechwan cuisine. There are several names for corn in Chinese, possibly because several varieties are known as well as because of dialect differences. Tiny ears of corn were easily adapted to the Chinese dishes of sliced mixed vegetables; as a result, in many parts of Canada these small ears of corn have come to be known as Chinese corn.

CURRY 咖喱 ga lei/k'a li

Curry powder, which is a mixture of various spices, usually including turmeric, originated in India and was introduced to China by traders. Many Cantonese dishes use curry powder, but a few differences should be noted between these curried dishes and Indian curries.

1. The curry spicing used in Chinese cooking is always ready-prepared, whereas dishes in Indian cuisine very frequently require different spice combinations for different dishes.
2. Chinese (and Japanese) cooks usually dry or burn the curry powder in a very hot pan before adding anything to it. The heat changes the color of the powder to a shade the Japanese call "fox-colored."
3. Chinese curries do not contain milk or butter; Indian curries sometimes do.
4. Chinese curries do not follow the authentic Indian practice of "cooking the dish to death"; the ingredients in the Chinese curries are still firm when served.

DOILIES. See Doughstuffs.

DOUGHSTUFFS

Wheat, rather than rice, is the staple of the northern Chinese diet, since the soil and climate of northern China are not suited to rice cultivation. Hence the doughstuffs of northern cooking are always made of wheat flour. Cantonese use both wheat and rice flours for a variety of dumplings and noodles.

Cantonese savory pastries, dumplings and noodles are generally available in special restaurants, so-called "noodle houses" or "pastry shops," and are typically eaten only at luncheon, at teatime, or as a late-evening snack. They are generally not available in regular restaurants, but even if they are, it is considered outré to order such dishes as part of a dinner meal. For this reason Cantonese doughstuff dishes have generally been excluded from this book. Spring Rolls, also called Egg Rolls, and Wonton have been excluded as well, since they too are in this special category.

On the other hand, northern restaurants in America, by which I mean restaurants other than Cantonese, usually list some type of dumpling and a few noodle dishes on the regular menu. Dumplings are eaten by the Chinese as appetizers in these restaurants even though at home these tempting tidbits, consumed by the dozens, form the entire meal. Noodles, if ordered as part of a meal, are generally eaten toward the end as rice usually is, but more often they are eaten alone as a light meal.

Except for noodles (see Noodles), the doughstuffs mentioned in this book are described below.

Dumpling Doilies are paper-thin discs of unleavened wheat-flour dough. They are used as dumpling skins and as wrappers for Peking Duck and Moo Shu Pork. When used with duck or pork, they are first griddle-fried. These fried discs, similar in appearance to tortillas, are called *bao pin/pao ping* (包 餅).

Dumplings (Wraplings) 餃 子 *chiao tzu* (Mandarin). Various mixtures are used as fillings for dumplings (see Szechwan Menu: Appetizers, Nos. 8, 9, 10), which may be boiled, steamed, or fried. When fried, they bear the descriptive Chinese name of "pot stickers" (鍋 貼 *wo tip/kuo t'ieh*).

Lotus Rolls (花 卷 *fa gün/hua chüan*) are also made of wheat-flour dough but with leavening (baking powder) added. Inch-thick circles of dough are indented with a fork around the edge and then steamed. During this time the dough puffs up and the creased edges curl so as to resemble a flower.

DUCK SAUCE

Two kinds of sauces are used by the Chinese as condiments for roast duck, and thus are known, particularly to Westerners, as duck sauce. One is the familiar sweet-tart variety commonly served in Chinese restaurants. It is a canned sauce made of plums, peaches, apricots, vinegar, and sugar, and is also called *plum sauce* (蘇梅醬 *so muey jeung/su mei jiang*).

Peking duck sauce, which is used for Peking duck, is not ready-prepared; it is a combination of *hoisin* sauce, grated orange rind, and sugar.

DUMPLING. See Doughstuffs.

EGG-FLOWERED 蛋花 *dan fa/tan hua*

"Egg-flowering" is the Chinese culinary practice of stirring raw egg into certain soups before they are served. The white, which is broken up by the stirring process and cooked by the hot soup, seems to resemble flower petals floating in the broth. The basic soup of this type is called "egg-drop" soup.

EGGS 蛋 *dan/tan*

Preserved Eggs 皮蛋 *pei dan/p'i tan*. Also called "ancient eggs" or "thousand-year eggs." The characters for this delicacy translate as "skin eggs," since the pastelike mixture with which the eggs (almost always duck eggs) are coated for preservation resembles a skin. The mixture consists of pinewood and charcoal ashes, lime, salt, and strong tea essence. After the eggs are thickly coated with the paste, they are placed in earthenware containers and covered with earth, where they are kept for at least 100 days. The water in the tea essence slakes the lime, thus producing heat that cooks the egg. As the aging process continues, the inside of the egg becomes increasingly firm, and the appearance of both yolk and white is altered. The transparent and jelly-like white becomes blue-black near the shell and lightens to amber color near the yolk. Depending upon the age of the egg, the yolk's color varies from brilliant yellow to vivid green.

Salted Eggs 鹹蛋 *ham dan/hsien tan*. Duck eggs are soaked in brine for thirty to forty days, during which time the white becomes salty and the yolk firm and bright orange. Eggs preserved in brine do not become "cooked" as the "thousand-year eggs" do. The yolk of the salted egg hardens because of dehydration effected by the saline solution, but the egg white remains runny. Salted eggs can be prepared in any way that fresh eggs might be, but of course the taste is completely different.

FISH 魚 yü/yü

> When the character for fish appears alone on a Cantonese menu, it usually means sea bass, whereas on the Szechwan menu, it generally refers to carp. To be sure, ask the waiter.

FISH, Salted 鹹魚 ham yü/hsien yü

> This is generally blowfish, flounder, or haddock that has been preserved by salting and drying. The flavor is extremely strong if the fish is eaten alone but less pungent when it is steamed with other meats, the way it is most often prepared.

FISH FLAVOR 魚香 yü hsiang (Mandarin only)

> Frequently used in Szechwan cuisine, this sauce is almost always translated on the menu as "garlic sauce." In my efforts to determine what is meant by the term "fish flavor," I have accumulated almost as many explanations as there are cures for hiccoughs. I list these bits of information on the subject.

1. "Fish flavor" is a combination of particular spices and flavorings that was originally used with fish, but is now used with many other foods.
2. "Fish flavor" is a flavored sauce whose base is fish stock.
3. "Fish flavor" is a term that is merely meant to recall a certain style of food preparation (as in the American expression "home-style cooking").
4. The oil that is used in "fish flavor" dishes is oil that has been used to fry fish or shrimp. This oil will then flavor the food.
5. The province of Szechwan, being landlocked, does not have salt-water fish. Therefore, bits of pork are substituted for fish, and the dish is called "fish-flavored."

Regardless of what is actually meant by "fish flavor," the following facts are valid for all dishes of this type:

1. The flavor is garlicky.
2. Hot bean paste or crushed red chili peppers are added in more than modest quantity.

3. Bits of chopped or shredded pork are included in these dishes.

FIVE-SPICE ESSENCE 五香粉 ng heung fun/wu hsiang fen
A frequently used seasoning consisting of star anise, fennel, cinnamon, cloves, and Szechwan pepper.

FLOUNDER 龍利 lung lei/lung li
Literally "dragon's tongue." The same characters are often used for sole as well.

FU JUNG 芙蓉 fu yung/fu jung
Fu jung (literally "hibiscus") dishes are so named because they are combined with beaten egg white, which puffs up so as to resemble the hibiscus flower. These elegant northern dishes have their counterparts in Cantonese cuisine. In the Cantonese version, however, both yolks and white are mixed with the other ingredients to make what is essentially an omelette. Although quite good, it is nonetheless considered to be a culinary condescension to Westerners.

Many Szechwan restaurants make authentic fu jung dishes, that is, using only whites in the preparation. Unfortunately, an increasing number are including the yolks as well, with the result that the "hibiscus" does not form.

FUNGUS, Tree 木耳 mook yee/mu erh (literally "wooden ear" or "tree ear"), or 雲耳 wun yee/yün erh (literally "cloud ear")
Tree fungi are mushroom-related parasitic plants that grow on tree stumps or trunks and protrude like little shelves or "ears." Some tree fungi are used as food by the Chinese, and are cultivated in China on cut oak saplings. Interestingly, European relatives of these fungi grow wild on elder exclusively, while in North America they are found on many deciduous trees.

One kind of tree fungus eaten by the Chinese is the

large, thick, and rather tough "wooden ear" or "tree ear," which also has some value in medicine as a cleansing or restorative agent. Another type, called "cloud ear" is smaller, softer, and considered more of a delicacy.

Although tree ears become limp when cooked, the texture is chewy, even resilient, a bit like some of the coarser seaweeds. The aristocratic mustiness of black Chinese mushrooms can also be detected in tree fungi, but to a lesser degree.

GARLIC SAUCE. See Fish Flavor.

GINGER 薑 geung/chiang

Ginger is the rhizome of a reedlike plant of the genus *Zingiber*. Although a rhizome is a fleshy stem that grows horizontally underground, the ginger rhizome is usually called a "root." Almost all ginger used in Chinese cooking is of the fresh or root form, which may be young, old, or pickled.

Young ginger (子 薑 *ji geung/tzu chiang*), also called green ginger, has tender, cream-colored skin and crunchy flesh that is tinged with pink and green. It has a delicate bouquet and a fresh, piquant flavor. Ordinarily the skin of young ginger is not removed for cooking purposes. As young ginger ages, the skin becomes pale brown and somewhat thicker. Although the ginger is still called "young," the flesh is coarser and the flavor is less subtle.

The term *old ginger* (生 薑 *saang geung/sheng chiang*) applies to mature ginger whose flesh, although tougher than that of young ginger, is not yet fibrous. Mature ginger has a sharp, biting taste that is very different from that of young ginger. When old ginger is used in cooking, the skin is generally pared, since it is rather tough and thick.

Pickled ginger (酸 薑 *sun geung/suan chiang*) is ginger root that has been preserved in spices, wine, and sugar. During the pickling process the root acquires a darker color and softer, more resilient texture. Its slightly sweet, winey flavor make it a perfect condiment for such rich-tasting dishes as preserved eggs.

GINKGO (*Gingko*) NUT 白菓 *bak go/pai kuo* (literally "white fruit")

    Ginkgo nuts are edible seeds of the fruit of an ancient tree, *Ginkgo biloba*, also called maidenhair tree. The fleshy part of the fruit is inedible, since it is foul-smelling and contains irritants that are chemically related to those in poison ivy. The pale buff-colored seeds, similar to almonds in appearance, are found in many Chinese dishes. When cooked, ginkgo seeds have a rather delicate nutlike flavor and pleasant mealy texture.

    The name "ginkgo" is taken from the old Japanese *gin kyo* (銀杏), which literally means "silver apricot." (In modern Japanese the word is *ginnan*.) Although the expression "white fruit" (白菓 *bak go/pai kuo*) is used for the ginkgo nut in both Mandarin and Cantonese speech, Mandarin also uses *yin hsing* (銀杏), which too means "silver apricot."

GOLDEN NEEDLES. See Lily Buds.

HAM 火腿 *fo tuy/huo t'ui*

    When ham is mentioned on a Chinese menu or in a recipe, the term always indicates a Smithfield-type product; that is, a rather heavily smoked and salted ham. There are a number of varieties, however, and the nuances of flavor vary. One such variety (金華 *gum wah/chin hua*, literally "golden flower") lends its name to the gourmet dish Golden Flower Jade Tree Chicken (see Cantonese Menu: Fowl, No. 38).

HOISIN SAUCE 海鮮醬 *hoi sin jeung/hai hsien chiang*

    A thick, dark sauce made of yellow soybeans, garlic, and spices, which is often mistaken for plum sauce. Although the taste is slightly sweet and fruity, almost plumlike, it is not the same as plum sauce. This error is frequently made by Chinese as well as Westerners. The characters for *hoisin*, which literally mean "sea taste sauce," has led to yet another false notion—that *hoisin* is made of fish. The fact is that it is meant to be a flavor *for* seafood. *Hoisin*,

a versatile sauce, is used not only as a condiment for seafood but for many other foods as well. It is also one of
the most ubiquitous flavoring ingredients in Chinese cuisine.

KETCHUP 茄汁   *fan keh jeung/fan ch'ieh chiang*

Ketchup, both the product and the word itself, has its
source in *koe tsiap*, a term meaning "fish brine" in the
Amoy dialect of Chinese. Although fish brine was a familiar food sauce in many Asian countries, the word *koe
tsiap*, or some form of it, came to be used for sauces other
than fish brine. For example, Indonesians call soy sauce
ketjap. The word "ketchup" has been used in England for
at least three centuries as the name for a thick, spicy
mushroom sauce. Eventually, many thick, variously flavored sauces came to be known as ketchup, including
the very American tomato ketchup.

Many Chinese dishes now use tomato ketchup as
an ingredient, but it is called either "tomato sauce"
(番茄醬 *fan keh jeung/fan ch'ieh chiang*) or "tomato juice" (番茄醬 *keh jap/ch'ieh chih*). It is a co-
incidence that the Cantonese phonetics for "tomato
juice" are very similar to *koe tsiap*, the original term.

KOHLRABI. See Preserved Vegetable.

LILY BUDS 金針 *gum jum/chin chen*

Literally "golden needles," these interesting delicacies are
really the buds of the day lily (genus *Hemerocallis*). They
are used either whole or shredded in various dishes, and
have a rather sweet-tart fruity taste. The day lily, so called
because its flower generally lasts just one day, is often
mistaken for the tiger lily since it has a similar orange
color.

LILY ROOT. See Lotus Root.

LOBSTER 龍蝦 *lung ha/lung hsia* (literally "dragon shrimp")

LOTUS LEAF ROLLS. See Doughstuffs.

LOTUS ROOT 蓮 藕 ling au/ou

The second character by itself means "lotus root" in Cantonese, but Cantonese menus use the first character for "lotus" as well. Lotus root is actually the fleshy stem (rhizome) of the sacred lotus (*Nelumbo*), a large aquatic plant symbolic of perpetual life in Buddhism. The lotus rhizomes grow horizontally (as do all rhizomes) in connected six-inch segments. They grow in the mud at water bottom and reach lengths of six or seven feet. The tuberous growth is largely carbohydrate and thus high in food value. Each segment has numerous "air tunnels" that resemble the holes in Swiss cheese when the segment is sliced crosswise. Cooked lotus stem has a crisp, crunchy texture and a deliciously nutty taste.

LOTUS SEED 蓮 子 ling ji/lien tzu

These edible seeds of the sacred lotus (*Nelumbo*) are found on the flat-topped receptacle which becomes visible when the lotus petals fall. The seeds are most often used in sweet dishes. Certain relatives of this lotus have produced seeds that were still viable after having been buried for 3,000 years.

MELON 瓜 gwa/kua

All the melons described below are true members of the gourd family (*Cucurbitaceae*). Unlike English, in which the word "melon" is restricted to sweet-tasting members of this family, the Chinese language refers to any member of the gourd family as a melon. Although the Chinese consume both sweet and savory types, only the latter are used in cooking.

Bitter Melon 苦 瓜 fu gwa/k'u kua. Also called balsam pear and bitter gourd, this dark-green, shiny-skinned melon (*Momordica charantia*) resembles a wrinkled cucumber. Acquiring a taste for its definitely bitter flavor may take some patience. In writing "bitter melon," the Chinese generally use the character for "bitter" (苦), but the Cantonese also use the term "cool" (凉 *leung*) melon, the latter being more acceptable to them, as they prefer to avoid words of unpleasant connotation.

Bottle Gourd Melon 葫 蘆 瓜 *pu lu gwa/hu lu kua.* A pear-shaped melon with smooth, pale-green skin, which is pared before the melon is cooked. The fresh-tasting, translucent flesh is used in soups and in dishes with chicken, pork, and beef.

Hair Melon 毛瓜 *mo gwa,* or 節瓜 *jit gwa* (Cantonese). Hair melon is a waxy-white, hair-covered gourd (*Benincasa hispida*), sometimes called Chinese watermelon, and has a thin, tough rind and tender, delicately flavored flesh, similar to that of the bottle gourd melon. Hair melon is found only in Cantonese dishes, never in other regional Chinese fare.

Ridged Melon 勝 瓜 *sing gwa/ssu kua.* This strange-looking cucumber-like gourd (*Tricosanthes anguina*), which grows on climbing plants, is variously called serpent, snake, or club gourd. Its tough, scaly skin, with lengthwise ridges, must be removed before the gourd is cooked. The pithy, almost spongelike flesh, usually used in soups, has a pleasantly bland taste. In Mandarin the characters for ridged melon 絲瓜 are frequently translated as silk melon, since the character 絲 can mean silk, thread, or fiber. A translation of fiber melon or thread melon would seem more accurate even if not so attractive, since the center of the gourd is fibrous rather than silky.

The word for "silk" in Cantonese dialect sounds like the word "to lose" (as in gambling); therefore the Cantonese menu always uses the character 勝 for this melon, since it means "to win."

The fibrous interior of ridged melon makes an excellent sponge when dried. In this dried state it is called a vegetable sponge or a luffa (or loofah), which is actually the name of its own botanical genus, *Luffa.*

Silk Melon. See Melon: *Ridged Melon.*

Tea Melon 茶 瓜 *chah gwa/ch'a kua.* Tea melon, used as a garnish for certain fish dishes or steamed with beef or pork, is a pickled delicacy made of certain small pale cucumbers, spices, wine, ginger, and honey. As the pickling process continues, the cucumbers darken until they become the color of tea—hence the name. In some sections of China the fresh cucumber is eaten, but it is still referred to as tea melon.

White Gourd Melon. See Melon: *Winter Melon.*

Winter Melon 冬 瓜 *dung gwa/tung kua.* Winter melon is a very large and smooth-skinned melon whose shape varies between round and slightly oblate. Although its skin is medium green, it is washed over with bloom, the white, frostlike coating also found on plums and grapes. The flesh of the melon is light green to white, and similar in appearance to that of its relative the honeydew.

The name winter melon derives from the fact that it is a variety of late-keeping musk melon, and is therefore stored for winter use. Its botanical name, *Cucumis melo inodorous,* distinguishes its odorless, bland-tasting flesh from the often fulsomely fragrant flesh of *Cucumis melo,* the musk melon. Unlike Western melon varieties, winter melon is never eaten raw. It is prepared in soups, and sometimes with chicken or shrimp. The dish for which it is best known is the sumptuous Winter Melon Cup (see Cantonese Menu: Soup, No. 19).

MONK'S FOOD. See Arhat's Feast.

MONOSODIUM GLUTAMATE (MSG) 味精 *mei jing/wei ching*
This white, crystalline salt ($C_5H_8O_4NaN$), sold under the trade names Ac'cent and Aji-no-Moto (Japanese), has been used for centuries by Chinese cooks. It is not a flavoring in itself, but rather a flavor enhancer that can be used with anything but sweets. Recently it has come under fire as the causative agent of "Chinese Restaurant Syndrome" (CRS), a group of symptoms including head-

ache, dizziness, and sweating, experienced by some people after dining in Chinese restaurants. As one who experiences a mild but almost immediate reaction to MSG, I have a few observations on the subject:

1. Soup with MSG seems to be the worst offender, possibly because the liquid dissolves the crystals more effectively.
2. Chinese restaurants catering to Westerners seem to use more of this substance than those that have a Chinese clientele.
3. The amount of MSG used varies from chef to chef. Since restaurants usually employ a few chefs, it is entirely possible that identical dishes in the same restaurant will be prepared with different quantities of MSG. If you are afflicted with the syndrome, tell the waiter that you don't want any MSG. To be on the safe side, show him the characters.

MUNG BEAN 綠豆 *luk dou/lü tou*

Mung (meng) beans are small green beans, not of the soybean group, used by Orientals in the preparation of soups, for the cultivation of bean sprouts, and for the manufacture of cellophane noodles (see Bean Thread).

MUSHROOMS 菇 *gu/ku*

The Chinese use mushrooms quite profusely in their cooking. *Button mushrooms* (蘑菇 *ma gu/ma ku*) are young field mushrooms and particularly evident in Westernized versions of Chinese dishes, although not all dishes containing these mushrooms are Westernized. The term "Chinese mushroom" refers generally to two kinds of dried mushroom. One is called *winter* (or *black*) *mushroom* (冬菇 *dung gu/tung ku*), a large, rather flat-topped growth; the other, more expensive *northern mushroom* (北菇 *bak gu/pei ku*) is smaller, with a speckled, more rounded cap. The Chinese also use *straw (grass) mushrooms* (草菇 *cho gu/ts'ao ku*), whose caps are small and shaped like pointed hats. These are usually canned but sometimes dried. (For a description of tree, cloud, and wooden ears, see Fungus, *Tree*.)

MUSTARD GREEN 芥菜 *gai choy/chieh ts'ai*
This is the same mustard green that is known in certain areas of America, but the Chinese are more diverse in their use of this dark-green, slightly bitter vegetable. It is used in soups, with sautéed beef or pork, or as a plain sautéed vegetable.

MUSTARD GREEN, *Pickled* 鹹菜 *ham choy/hsien ts'ai*
Literally "salted vegetable," pickled mustard greens are also known as pickled cabbage, Chinese sauerkraut, and Chinese mustard pickle. In the preparation of this salted vegetable, fresh mustard greens are pickled in barrels with salt, wine, and a touch of sugar—a process that eliminates the sharpness of the fresh green and imparts to it a tart-sweet flavor. Young pickled mustard greens—those that have been in brine for a short time—are crunchy, sweet-sour in flavor and darkish green in color. As the pickling process continues, the leaves become lighter and the stalks softer. The flavor of these mature greens is sour-salty rather than sweet-sour. Young greens are available in autumn and early winter, while the mature greens are a year-round item. Both are excellent with beef and pork and in soup.

NOODLES: *Drawn Noodles* 撈麵 *loh min/lao mien*

Rice-Flour Noodles 米粉 *mai fen/mi fen*

Wheat-Flour Noodles 麵 (條) *min/mien* (hao)
The Chinese use many kinds of noodles as the basic ingredient for a veritable panorama of dishes. Special noodle houses offer the best prepared and most impressive selec-

tion of such dishes. Wheat and rice flours are used for the dough, which is cut into many sizes and shapes. Chinese enjoy this fare at lunchtime or as a late snack, but never with a full dinner. Drawn noodles are the familiar *lo mein*, made of wheat-flour dough that is worked by being pulled or drawn. For *cellophane, bean starch,* and *pea-starch noodles,* see Bean Thread.

OIL

Soybean oil is the most widely used cooking oil in China, but the Chinese in America more frequently use peanut oil, cottonseed oil, or lard. For family cooking and general restaurant use, peanut oil is almost always the choice, since its own flavor never interferes with the taste of the other ingredients. Sesame oil is used as a flavoring for soups and other dishes. If chicken oil (i.e., chicken fat, 鶏 油 *gai yau/chi yu*) is used in the preparation of a dish, it is identified on the menu, as in Carp with Chicken Fat. Red pepper oil (辣 油 *la yau/la yu*), also called red-hot oil in Szechwan cuisine, is used both in cooking and as a table condiment, particularly in Szechwan restaurants. It is made of peanut oil in which red peppers have been fried. Butter is rarely used in Chinese cooking, and olive oil never.

OYSTER SAUCE 蠔 油 ¹*ho yau/hao yu*

This is a thick sauce made of oyster extract, water, salt, cornstarch, and caramel coloring. It is used in Chinese dishes to impart a deep, rich flavor to sauces and meats, but it does not have the fishy flavor that its name implies. Also served as a dip with some dishes.

PEANUTS 花生 *fa saang/hua sheng*

This name for peanuts has been shortened from 落花生 *lau fa saang/lo hua sheng*, which literally means "seeds from flowers that have fallen to the ground."

PEAS, *Green* 青豆 ching dou/ch'ing tou
When green peas are mentioned on a Chinese menu, they are pea *kernels*, not snow peas.

PEKING SAUCE 京醬 ching chiang (Mandarin)
Peking sauce, a combination of *hoisin* sauce and brown bean sauce frequently used in Szechwan cuisine, imparts a slightly sweet taste and pleasantly musty aroma to dishes. It is used only as a flavoring, never as a condiment or dip.

PEPPER

The word "pepper" is misleading, since it is usually used to encompass more than it should. Certain peppers belong to the true family, while others are members of unrelated plants. The Chinese use many kinds of pepper belonging to these various categories. The most frequently used are named below with some brief botanical comments.

Black Pepper and *White Pepper* are the berries of the true pepper plant, a tropical shrub called *Piper nigrum*. Black pepper is the dried berry of this shrub, while white pepper is the ripe berry with its hull removed. White pepper is milder than black, since removal of the hull also removes certain acrid resins that give the pepper berry its pungency. In China, cooks use more white pepper than black, while in America the opposite is usually true. A good example is Sour and Hot Soup (see Szechwan Menu: Soup, No. 1), which is made with white pepper in China, but more often with black pepper in the States.

Bell Peppers or Sweet Peppers (青椒 ching ju/ch'ing chiao), a variety of *Capsicum frutescens*, are unrelated to *Piper nigrum*, the pepper shrub. *Capsicum frutescens* belongs to the nightshade family (*Solanaceae*), which includes tomatoes, eggplant, and potatoes.

Chili Peppers or *Red Peppers* (辣椒 la ju/la chiao) are another variety of *Capsicum frutescens*. These fruits are used in abundance by Szechwan chefs but only rarely by Cantonese. The hotness of these peppers is caused by a water-insoluble acidic substance contained within the inner membrane of the pod.

Szechwan Pepper (花椒 *fa ju/hua chiao*), literally "flower pepper," is used as a spice and condiment in almost all regions of China. It is the deep scarlet fruit of a tall shrub called Japanese or Chinese pepper, native to eastern Asia. The botanical name of this plant is *Xanthoxylum piperitum* of the order *Rutaceae*, the same order to which citrus fruits belong. Szechwan pepper, despite its name and dark-red color, is not at all hot; it has an aromatic flavor, similar to that of cardamom.

A good deal of confusion in nomenclature exists among the various peppers used in Chinese cooking. Since Szechwan pepper is red, it is often translated as "red pepper," and since the little dried fruits resemble peppercorns, it is often called "black pepper." To confound the matter further, chili peppers, used so abundantly in Szechwan cooking either whole or shredded, are frequently and erroneously referred to as "Szechwan pepper."

PORK 豬肉 *jyu yuk/chu jou*

Pork is the most frequently used meat in Chinese cuisine. The characters literally mean "pig meat." Whenever the second character 肉 (meat) is used by itself on a menu, it always means pork.

PORK, Roast 义燒 *chah shu/chu shao*

The well-known Chinese roast pork—or barbecued pork, as it is also called—is made of lean pork loin that is first rubbed with salt, pepper, five-spice essence, sugar, sherry, and soy, then oven-roasted. While it is in the oven it is based with its own drippings so that the outside becomes a rich mahogany color.

The Chinese characters for this dish literally mean "fork roasted" or "fork barbecued." Although originally a cooking method for any meat, it has come to be synonymous with roast pork.

PRESERVED VEGETABLE

All sections of China preserve some type of cabbage or turnip. Most of these preserved vegetables have their own distinctive flavors, and are peculiar to the area where they were preserved. Salted vegetables (鹹 菜 *ham choy/hsien ts'ai*) may be any of several kinds of cabbage or turnip. In this book, however, the term salted vegetable indicates pickled mustard green (see Mustard Green, *Pickled*). Four other kinds of preserved vegetable included in the dishes presented in this book are described below.

Canton Preserved Vegetable (廣東冲菜 *gwang dung chong choy*) is made of kohlrabi or *bok choy*. The leaves and stalks of the vegetable are wrapped into a tight head and then marinated in garlic and pepper. It is almost never used in Chinese cuisines other than Cantonese, where the name is always shortened to 冲菜 (*chong choy*) on the menu. Usually served with beef or pork, it has a hot and garlicky flavor.

Szechwan Preserved Vegetable (四川榨菜 *sei ch'uen jya choy/ssu ch'uan cha ts'ai*), also called Szechwan cabbage or preserved turnip, is really the stem of the kohlrabi plant. This fleshy bulbous stem, which resembles a turnip, is left whole and dry-preserved in salt, spices, and red pepper. The resulting flavor is hot and aromatic. Featured on both Szechwan and Cantonese menus with beef, with pork, and in soup, its name is always simplified to 榨菜 (*jya choy/cha ts'ai*). Quite paradoxically, it is somewhat less spicy in Szechwan than in Cantonese dishes because Szechwan cooks remove more of the pepper preservative.

Ta T'ou Ts'ai (才頭菜) literally means "big-head vegetable" and is a type of preserved kohlrabi used only in northern cuisine. Whole kohlrabi stem, preserved in dark soy, salt, and spices, becomes very salty and almost black. When cooked it has a rather fruity flavor.

Tientsin Winter Vegetable (天津冬菜 *tin jeun dung choy/t'ien chin tung ts'ai*) is made of shredded celery cabbage that has been heavily seasoned with garlic, then packed in earthenware pots and sealed. As the cabbage ferments it develops the strong salty flavor that becomes the basis for many hearty home-style dishes. Although used by Chinese other than Cantonese, it is listed only on Cantonese menus, where it is abbreviated to 冬 菜 (*dung choy/tung ts'ai*).

RICE: Cooked 飯 fahn/fan

Fried 炒飯 chau fahn/ch'ao fan

Potted 煲飯 bo fahn (Cantonese)

Uncooked 白米 bak mai/pai mi

Rice is the most important grain product of China. So basic is its presence in the Chinese diet that the characters for breakfast, luncheon, and dinner translate literally as "early rice," "midday rice," and "evening rice," respectively.

Although less important than maize and wheat in the north and northeast, it is the predominant crop in southern and southwestern China. As a consequence, enormous quantities of rice are consumed in the southern province of Canton. It may be simply boiled, or the main ingredient of fried rice and potted rice dishes.

Fried rice, one of the most popular items of Chinese food among Westerners, is not eaten as ordinary fare by the Chinese themselves. It is a banquet dish that often replaces the bowls of boiled white rice at such dinners. For this reason, and because they are so well known to Westerners, fried rice dishes have not been included in this guide.

Potted Rice (see Cantonese Menu: Potted Rice) originated as a simple, inexpensive one-dish meal for laborers. Prepared in earthenware pots, these rice dishes with small pieces of meat were eaten at noonday or suppertime. Potted rice is available in some Cantonese restaurants in the larger American cities, but metal vessels usually replace the earthenware pots and the quantity of meat added is greater.

Although potted rice dishes technically fall into the category of special dishes, a few have been listed in the guide, since most Westerners are completely unfamiliar with this unpretentious fare.

SAUSAGE   *Duck Liver Sausage* 鴨肝腸 opp gan chong/ya (tzu) kan chiang

Pork Sausage 惜腸 lap chong/la chiang
There are two kinds of Chinese sausage—one made of ground pork and spices, and the other of duck liver and spices. A bit of sugar is added to both kinds. These sausages are rather thin and have a firm, almost brittle consistency similar to that of pepperoni. Duck liver sausage is very rich, and therefore rarely eaten alone. It is usually served with slices of pork sausage. The unusual, faintly sweet flavor of either type is delicious with *choy sum* or with arrowhead tuber.

SCALLION 葱 chung/ts'ung
When this character appears on a Chinese menu, it may stand for either scallions or leeks.

SEA CUCUMBER 海参 hoi sum/hai shen
This protein-rich marine animal, also called *bêche-de-mer*, trepang, and sea slug, is a warty-skinned creature belonging to the starfish phylum (*Holothurioida echinodermata*). The name *bêche-de-mer*, which means "sea spade" in French, is derived from the digging and scooping movements it effects while feeding on the sea bottom. The sea cucumber is highly regarded as a delicacy in the Orient, and about twenty-four species, ranging in size from six inches to more than two feet, are collected for food. In some countries their production and protection are government-supervised.

Marine biologists have known for some time that this

ancient creature has the ability to synthesize opal. Moreover, it was discovered recently that the sea cucumber also
synthesizes beads of iron under its skin (*New York
Times*, May 8, 1975). The use of these substances to the
animal has not yet. been determined. The vaguely me-
dicinal flavor and slippery, rubbery texture of the sea cucumber are alien to Western tastes; nonetheless, it should
be tried by anyone interested in Chinese cuisine. A good
introduction would be Sea Cucumber and Abalone Soup
(Cantonese Menu: Soup, No. 17).

SEAWEED

Although many kinds of seaweed (algae) are used in Chinese cooking, hair seaweed and laver are the only two
used in the dishes described in this book. Hair seaweed
(髮 菜 *fat choy/fa ts'ai*), named for its long hairlike
strands, is extremely expensive, and therefore any dish
containing it is also expensive. The phonetics for its characters are the same as the phonetics for the characters
meaning "may you become rich," the customary Chinese
New Year greeting. Consequently, dishes prepared with
hair seaweed have special significance during the lunar
New Year.

Laver (紫 菜 *ji choy/tzu ts'ai*) grows in the form
of translucent purple-red fronds. These are harvested,
dried, and compressed into cakes, which are used in soups
and other dishes. Laver is much less costly than hair seaweed and can be enjoyed the year around.

SHARK'S FIN

魚 翅 *yü jih/yü ch'ih*

The cartilage of the shark's fin (a shark has a skeleton of
cartilage rather than of bone) is removed and soaked in
water for several hours until it is soft. The long gelatinous
threads are then used in the well-known Shark's Fin Soup
(Szechwan Menu: Soup, No. 6) and in other dishes.
Shark's fin has little flavor by itself but combines well with
other ingredients. Since the fins themselves are in short
supply and their preparation is time-consuming, dishes
containing shark's fin are expensive. Banquets and other
special affairs almost always include a shark's fin dish.

SNAILS 石螺 *syet lo/shih lo*

The small, blue-black snails consumed by Cantonese are really periwinkles—sea snails that cling to rocks along the intertidal shore zone. They are daintier than the French *escargots,* which are large, grayish-white land snails, but every bit as delicious, particularly when prepared, as they usually are, in a spicy-hot black bean sauce.

SNOW PEAS 雪豆 *syut dou/hsüeh tou*

Also called sugar peas, *pois mange-tout, mange-tout,* or simply peapods, snow peas are a separate sort of pea whose pod has no parchment lining such as that of shelling peas. In most sections of China this vegetable is called the Holland pea (荷蘭豆 *ho lan dou/ho lan tou*), but the people of Canton province who speak the Toisan dialect call them snow peas, and since the majority of Cantonese restaurateurs in New York speak the Toisan dialect, the term snow peas is the more widely used in New York. I have not been able to determine why the terms snow peas or Holland peas are used at all.

SOUP

Generally the character 湯 (*tang/t'ang*) is used for soup on the Chinese menu. This means that the base of the soup is some ready-prepared broth, bouillon, or stock, or a combination of fresh and canned preparations. Another expression for soup (上湯 *seung tang/shang t'ang*) signifies that only the freshly prepared, long-cooked broth of chicken, beef, pork, or some other meat or fish has been used. The latter type of soup is usually featured as special or banquet fare.

SOY PEA. See Soybean.

SOY SAUCE 醬油 *jeung yau/chiang yu*

Fermentation of soybeans in brine, a process that takes eight to twelve months, is the traditional method of making soy sauce in the Orient. In the United States, the use of a much quicker method, acid hydrolysis, results in a generally inferior-tasting product. Although almost all Far Eastern countries use some type of soy sauce in cooking, these sauces vary noticeably in taste. The Chinese produce and use several kinds of soy sauce, each having a distinctive flavor, thickness, and use.

The only two that are pertinent to the dishes in this book are the usual dark soy, also called heavy soy (老 抽 *lo chau/lao ch'ou*), found on tables of many Chinese restaurants, and a much paler one (生 抽 *saang chau/sheng ch'ou*), translated as light or thin soy. The former is a heavy cooking soy such as that used in red-cooked dishes; the latter is used as a flavoring ingredient. Chinese never use soy sauce, salt, or pepper while dining, except as a dip with dumplings, as this is considered an unflattering reflection upon the chef. The only condiments used by the Chinese are the white vinegar and red-hot oil often found in dispensing bottles on the tables, or a dip that accompanies some particular dish.

Many Chinese restaurants now place an all-purpose Japanese soy on the table, but regardless of the kind, the soy sauce is there for Westerners, some of whom put it on everything but the fortune cookies.

SOYBEAN 黃大豆 *wang tai dou/huang ta tou*

From among the many kinds of legumes used in the Orient, the soy (or soya) bean is perhaps the most familiar to Westerners. Known also as China bean, Japanese pea, soy pea, or white gram, the soybean is one of the five sacred grains of the Oriental religions, the others being rice, wheat, barley, and millet. Soybean cultivation dates back as far as the second millennium B.C. Seeds of the soy plant are usually yellow, green, brown, or black, but may be bicolored. There are many yellow-seeded varieties in the Orient; in fact, the literal translation of the Chinese characters for soybean is "yellow big bean." No truly white or red seeds are known.

Soybeans have more balanced protein than any other vegetable crop. (A balanced protein is one that contains adequate amounts of the amino acids essential to humans.) The protein of soybeans is almost equivalent to animal protein, even containing lysine, an amino acid only infrequently found in plants. Thus soybeans and their derived products are excellent meat substitutes and meat supplements. A complete amino acid analysis of soybean protein shows it to be similar to casein, the chief protein of milk. One of the essential amino acids in which soybeans are deficient is methionine. Recent work in soybean tissue culture is aimed toward the correction of this deficiency. Ways to increase the proportion of urease, an enzyme rich in methionine, are being studied.

SPARERIBS 排骨 *pai gwat* (not a Szechwan dish)

SQUIRREL FISH 松鼠魚 *sung shu yü* (Mandarin)
Squirrel fish is not a type of fish but rather a Chinese pun on the sounds of the first two characters. Originally this boneless sweet and sour fish was prepared with pine nuts and thus was called pine nut fish. In certain dialects of Chinese, the word for pine nut is a homonym of squirrel.

STAR ANISE 八角 *bat goh/pa chiao*
Also called Chinese anise, this lovely seasoning is the licorice-scented fruit (not a seed) of an evergreen shrub (*Illicum verum*) grown in China. The fruit clusters, in the shape of eight-pointed stars, are aptly described by their Chinese characters, which mean "eight corners." The more familiar aniseed is a member of the carrot family and thus not related to star anise, although the two are somewhat similar in flavor. Star anise is used frequently but sparingly in various dishes and is also one of the spices of *Five-Spice Essence*.

STRING BEAN 豆仔 *dou jai* (Cantonese); 扁豆 *p'ien tou* (Mandarin)

Also in Mandarin: 四季豆 ssu *chi tou* (literally "four-season vegetable")

> In addition to the familiar string bean, Chinese use a related long green bean called a Chinese string bean (豆角 *dou goh/tou chiao*, literally "bean corner"). It is thinner and crunchier than the Western variety, and about a foot long.

SWEET AND SOUR 甜酸 *tim sün/t'ien suan*

> Sweet and sour sauce, as the name implies, is a blend of sweet and tart ingredients, such as sugar and vinegar or pineapple juice and sweet pickle juice. In sweet-sour Szechwan dishes ketchup is often added to the sauce, which then has a bright reddish color. Sweet and sour sauce is used in many dishes, perhaps the most famous of which is Sweet and Sour Pork (Cantonese Menu: Pork, No. 23).

SWIM BLADDER 鱼肚 *yü tou/yü tu*

> This pale, puffy, translucent substance seen hanging in windows of Chinese groceries is the swim bladder of the conger, a large marine eel. A swim bladder is an air-filled sac by means of which a fish raises and lowers itself in the water. Chinese deep-fry the conger swim bladder until it expands to several times its deflated size. Then it is broken up and served in certain soups, where it assumes the texture of a pleasantly soft dumpling. It has absolutely no fishy taste. The Chinese expression 鱼肚 incorrectly identifies the swim bladder as fish belly. Two equally incorrect but frequent translations are fish maw and fish tripe.

SZECHWAN CABBAGE. See Preserved Vegetable: Szechwan Preserved Vegetable.

TEA 茶 *chah/ch'a*

> Tea is a product of the dried and prepared leaves of *Thea*

sinensis, an evergreen shrub that is cultivated in China, Japan, and India, as well as in other places where a warm, damp climate prevails. Irrespective of the type of tea—green or black—the leaves have been gathered from the same tea shrub. Processing of the leaves, however, varies according to the desired flavors and aromas.

The many kinds of tea, including Chinese teas, which number almost three hundred, fall more or less into three groups: (1) black teas, also called fermented; (2) green teas, also called unfermented; and (3) semifermented.

Black teas are called "red teas" by the Chinese because of the amber or reddish color of the infusion. In the processing of black teas, the leaves, after being picked, are allowed to wither and ferment slightly before being dried. Green teas consist of young leaves that have been quickly dried without being fermented. In the processing of semifermented teas, the leaves are only partially fermented before they are dried. The chemical change that takes place during fermentation is essentially oxidation of the tannin. Oxidase, an enzyme present in the leaf, is the catalyst for this oxidation.

Oolong tea (literally "black dragon"), a semifermented type, is the one most frequently served in Chinese restaurants in America. Scented teas, such as jasmine tea and chrysanthemum tea, sometimes accompany elaborate luncheons or banquets. These scented teas are oolong and green teas flavored with the petals of flowers. Lapsang Souchang, another rather familiar tea, is a smoked black tea with a distinctive smoky flavor.

TOP SHELL 响螺 *heung lo/hsiang lo*

Top shell, a rather large mollusk whose shell is in the form of a tightly spiraled top, is one of the more unfamiliar ingredients of Chinese cuisine. It is frequently referred to as conch, and often conch *is* substituted for it. The two mollusks belong to different genera, however (conch to *Strombus,* top shell to *Trochidae*), and are distinct from each other in size, taste, and texture. Top shell is smaller than conch and has a more refined texture and delicate taste.

VEGETABLE HEART. See Cabbage Heart.

WATER CHESTNUT 馬蹄 mah tai/ma t'i (literally "horse's hoof")

There are many edible water chestnuts. None are related to the tree-grown chestnut, and only a few are related to each other. Chinese of almost all regions use at least one kind of water chestnut in cooking; these may be used as a vegetable or dried and ground into a flour. Regardless of the type, most Chinese call them "horse's hoof," a name derived from their general shape and dark exterior.

Two of the water chestnuts found in Chinese markets are the nutlike fruit of a group of floating aquatic plants belonging to the genus *Trapa*. Native to Asia, these plants are related to the evening primrose family. One of the fruits, *Trapa natans*, has four prongs or horns, and is also called water caltrop. Another species, whose fruit has two long horns, is the *Trapa bicornis*.

A group of rushlike plants (*Eleocharis*) yields a third kind of water chestnut that is widely eaten by Orientals. This type, however, rather than being the fruit of the plant, is an edible corm. (A corm is the large, fleshy, bulblike base of a certain kind of stem.) When seen in markets, these water chestnuts look very much like narcissus bulbs. Mandarin-speaking people sometimes call them *pi ch'i* (荸 薺) as well as *ma t'i*.

Early American Indians along the eastern coast consumed yet another kind of water chestnut, called water chinquapin. These are edible nutlike seeds of the American lotus, *Nelumbo lutea*.

WATERCRESS 西洋菜 sai yang choy/hsi yang ts'ai (literally "western vegetable")

WINTER VEGETABLE. See Preserved Vegetable: *Tientsin Winter Vegetable.*

YELLOW BEAN

The source of brown bean paste (面 豉 *meen see/ mien ch'ih*) and brown bean sauce (面 豉 汁 *meen see jap/mien ch'ih chih*). The paste is made of crushed, salted yellow beans and is used as a preservative, while the sauce, a slightly sweet, thick, reddish-brown purée, consists of bean paste to which sugar and spices have been added. The sauce is used to season fish, fowl, and meat dishes, particularly in Szechwan cuisine, and has a taste and texture somewhat like those of peanut butter.

Flavors added to brown bean paste and sauce vary according to the section of origin. For example, hot bean paste, a specialty of Szechwan province, is a combination of yeollow bean paste and crushed red chili peppers.

Appendix

cHiNESE pRONUNCiATiON
ANd NUMbERS

PHONETICS SYSTEM~CANTONESE

The system used here has been devised after listening as carefully as possible to patient Cantonese-speaking friends and acquaintances. The multitoned Cantonese dialect with its glottal stops and vowel clusters, unfamiliar to most speakers of American English, makes the task of reproducing the sounds a formidable one. Among the Cantonese themselves accents vary considerably. Moreover, there is no substantial agreement among experts on pronunciation standards. The representations given below of the Cantonese transcriptions used in this guide can therefore be only middling approximations of the actual sounds, and untrained readers are advised not to attempt to order in Cantonese.

Vowels are similar to those of the Romance languages; long vowels (either written with a superimposed line, as in *chō*, or doubled, as in *saang*) are merely given double value. Words with *uy* in them sound like the diphthongs in French *feuilles* and *trompe l'oeil*; if you are not familiar with this French sound, pronounce "toy" in English with very pursed lips for a close resemblance. Words with *eun* rhyme roughly with "burn" and "learn," drawn out and pronounced without the r, as in Oxford English. The sound of ung should resemble the final syllable of the German achtung. The umlauted ü is pronounced as in German über and French une. Although glottal stops pepper the English of Scottish, Cockney, Australian, and northeastern American colloquial speech, they are not recognized as such by the average English speaker. Glottal stops in our language can be heard in "backgammon"; in some New Yorkers' "bottle" ("bah-uhl"); in a Scot's pronunciation of Scotland; and in the very American "Uh-uh!" For our purposes, though, these stops are noted here with an asterisk (*) and a close approximation of sounds that should be glided together. Unless otherwise indicated, the sounds are taken from standard American speech, and are identified here with boldface.

au	ouch	fen	funny
bak*	as in boxer, bok*-ser	fo	folks
ban	bond	fu	phooey!
bao	take a bow	fung	fungus
bat*	bot*-tle	ga	garbage
bau	take a bow	gai	guy
beun	British burn	gan	gondola
bo	bo peep	geung	British gurgle + sing
cha	Spanish muchacha	go	gopher
chah	charge	goh	goal
chai	chide	gu	ghoul
chang	Charles + sing	guk*	go + look*
chau	chow	gük*	go + look*, umlauted
ching	munching	gum	goombay
chit*	chit*	gün	gun, umlauted
cho	choke	gwa	aw, g'wan!
chō	Spanish mucho with an American accent	gwai	Goldberg, why?
chong	choke + aw + song	gwang	aw, g'wan! + bong
choy	choice	gwat*	Goldberg, what?
chung	chop + look + song	ha	holly
chün	chew, umlauted, + noun	hai	hyacinth
dan	Donald	ham	hominy grits
dik*	Dick*called	han	Honduras with an American accent
ding	ding-a-ling	hang	honky-tonk
dou	dough	heen	heel + noun
dun	done	heung	British heard + sing
dung	do(i)ng	ho	hope
fa	father	hoi	hoity-toity
faai	father + yeast	hop*	hup*-2-3-4!
fahn	bouffant	hung	hook + song
fan	phenomenon	jaang	John + song

jai	July	pai	python
jap*	job + Nop*e!	pei	pay
jau	jowl	pin	penalize
jeun	British journey	pu	poodle
jeung	British journey + song	saang	sop + sing
ji	Jeep	sai	sigh
jih	gee whiz	sam	somber
jin	gin	sap*	sop*
jing	Jean gave me	see	see
jit*	legit*imate	seung	British discern + sing
jong	jonquil	shu	shoo-fly
ju	Jupiter	sih	see
juk*	juke*-box	sik*	sick*
jum	jump	sin	seen
jung	jukebox + song	sing	receiving
jya	gee whiz + on	siu	see + chew
jyu	gee whiz + you	soong	Susan + sing
kao	cow	sui	sway
kap*	cop*per	sum	summa cum laude
keh	Kenneth	süm	sum, umlauted
kin	king	sun	person
la	la-dee-dah	sün	sun, umlauted
lan	Lonny	sut*	suit*yerself!
lap*	lop*sided	syet*	it's yet* to come
lau	lousy	sying	seen + sing
lei	lazy	syu	see + you
leng	lung	syut*	see y't*night
leung	British learn + sing	tai	Thailand
li	leap	tang	ice tongs
ling	darling	ti	tea
lo	lost	tim	team
loh	low	tin	sateen
lu	Lucy	ting	sateen + sing
luk*	look*	tip*	tip*
lung	look + song	tou	toe
mah	mama	tun	tundra
mai	my	tuy	French argenteuil
meen	mean	yan	yonder
mei	may	yang	Yonkers
min	mince	yat*	yacht*
ming	seeming	yau	yowl
mook*	man + look*	yee	yeast
mu	moo	yeung	British yearn + sing
mun	mundane	yi	ye
ng	sing	yih	yippee!
nga	sing on	yin	playin'
ngau	sing out	yu	you
nam	nominate	yü	you, umlauted
opp*	pop*-up	yuk*	you + look*

yun	you + Spanish uno	wang	Wankel engine
yün	you + French une	wat*	swat*
yung	you + song	wo	war
yut*	you + foot*prints	wu	wounded
wah	wasp	wun	wonderful
wai	Wyoming		

PHONETICS SYSTEM ~ MANDARIN

The system used is according to Wade-Giles. Unless otherwise indicated, the approximated sounds of the English examples are those of standard American speech. Make certain to pronounce the English equivalents as one would in ordinary colloquial speech, running the sounds together. Letters to be pronounced are in boldface. Some of the sounds are impossible to approximate in English. The sound of the letter h (except when followed by s) is guttural, much like that of the Castilian j. H followed by s is slightly aspirated, as in this *sh*eep. The letter j is somewhat like the sound Americans make in the r of row, but if you can make it sound something like *zh*row, you will be closer to the actual Mandarin. Any word ending in ung should be pronounced as the Germans pronounce the ung in Nibelung. The umlauted ü is prounced as in German über or in French une. This is not a complete listing of Mandarin phonetics; only those used in this guide are given.

cha	John	ching	Jean gave me
ch'a	Charles	ch'ing	munching
chang	jonquil	ch'iu	how much she owe yuh?
ch'ang	chop + bong	ch'ou	choke
ch'ao	chow	chu	Jupiter
che	just	chüan	did you enter?
chen	just + sun	ch'uan	how much yuh want?
ch'en	chump + sun	ch'un	which one?
cheng	junkyard	erh	are you?
chi	gee whiz	fa	father
ch'i	cheap	fan	bouffant
chia	geology	fen	funny
chiang	geology + sing	feng	fungus
chiao	geology + ouch	fu	fooled
chieh	geology + echo	hai	hydrant
ch'ieh	much yellow	hao	how
chien	geology + enter	ho	hole
chih	jerk	hsi	sheep
ch'ih	chirp	hsia	she opted
chin	bluejeans	hsiang	she Yonkers

hsiao	she yowled	ou	owe
hsieh	she entered	pa	Sparta
hsien	she entered	pai	spyglass
hsin	sheen	p'an	part + Tonto
hsing	sheen goes	pang	bong
hsü	she you	pao	take a bow
hsüeh	she you enter	pei	baby
hu	who	pi	beetle
hua	h + qualify	p'i	peace
huang	h + Wankel engine	p'in	penalize
hui	h + wait	p'ien	Peter entered
hung	h + ung(Ger.Nibelung)	pu	bully
huo	h + whoa	san	it's on the table
i	reap	se	sir
jen	run	sha	shah of Iran
jou	row	shang	shah + song
ju	rouge	shao	shower
jung	r + ung(Ger.Nibelung)	sheng	nation + rung
k'a	coddle	shih	Shirley
kan	gondola	shu	shoo-fly
ke	girl	shuang	shoo, on, + sing
ku	goof	shui	sh + wait
k'u	coop	ssu	psssst + us
kua	Gowanus	su	sue
kuai	Goldberg, why?	suan	Sue entered
k'uai	quiet	sui	sway
kung	gold + ung (Ger.Nibelung	sun	sun + Spanish uno*
kuo	baby talk, gwow up (grow up)	sung	sun + ung (Ger.Nibelung)
la	tra-la	ta	start
lao	lousy	t'ai	Thailand
lan	longitude	tan	Donald
li	leap	t'ang	ice tongs
lien	Lee entered	t'ao	tower
lin	lean	t'i	tea
liu	Lee owes me	t'ieh	tea yellow
lo	lo and behold	t'ien	tea entered
lu	Lucy	ting	ding-a-ling
lü	lieu	tou	do-re-mi
lung	let + ung(Ger.Nibelung)	t'ou	toe
ma	mama	ts'ai	it sighed
mi	me	ts'ao	Rhett's sow
mien	me enter	ts'u	it soothed
ming	me + sing	tsui	did sway
mu	moo	ts'ui	it sways
nai	deny	ts'ung	its + ung(Ger.Nibelung)
nan	hey-nonny-nonny	tu	do you?
niu	knee yoke	t'u	two

t'ui	baby talk, **twaipse** (traipse)	wu	**woo**
		ya	**Yonkers**
t'un	baby talk, **twundle** (trundle)	yan	yonder
		yang	**Yonkers**
tung	**dog + ung** (Ger.Nibel-ung)	yao	yowl
		yen	wee'**un**
tzu	**dz + us**	yin	you + **bean**
tz'u	**tz + us**	you	yokel
wan	**want**	yu	**you**
wei	**wait**	yü	you, umlauted
wo	**water**	yün	you, umlauted, + now

NUMBERS

Two kinds of characters are used for prices on Chinese menus. Ordinary Chinese numerals appear on the standard menu along with the characters for the dishes. Both are usually typeset. For additions to the standard menu, particularly in Cantonese restaurants, pink sheets are inserted in the menu or pink strips of paper are affixed to the restaurant wall. On these, the prices are given in handwritten Soochow figures.

Both types of figures, and samples of the monetary counting system using ordinary Chinese numerals, are shown below. Samples of the handwritten Soochow figures are not given since they are less frequently used and are not easily recognized by the inexperienced.

Although phonetics for the terms are also designated, it is not advisable to verbalize them should questions arise about the prices, since, especially among the Cantonese, quite different expressions are sometimes used in the spoken language.

ARABIC	ORDINARY	SOOCHOW	CANTONESE	MANDARIN
1	一	/	yat	i
2	二	刂	yi	erh
3	三	川	sam	san
4	四	Ⅹ	sei	ssu
5	五	8	ng	wu
6	六	㇒	luk	liu
7	七	㇒	chat	ch'i
8	八	㇒	bat	pa
9	九	夊	gau	chiu
10	十	十	suhp	shih
Dollar	元		yün	yüan
Dime	毫	毛	hou	mao
	(Cantonese)	(Mandarin)		

SAMPLES

(a)　二 = two
　　元 = dollars ⎫
　　五 = five ⎬ $2.50
　　毫 = dimes ⎭

(c)　一 = one
　　元 = dollars ⎫
　　七 = seven ⎬ $1.75
　　五 = five ⎭

(b)　九 = nine ⎫
　　五 = five ⎬ 95¢
　　毫 = dimes ⎭

(d)　三 = three ⎫
　　元 = dollars ⎬ $3.00

Indexes

THE SZECHWAN MENU

DOROTHY FARRIS LAPIDUS studied Chinese at New York University and Columbia. As a diversion she began to translate the Chinese-language menu of a Cantonese restaurant, and soon realized that the menu was a discipline in itself.

Mrs. Lapidus is the wife of Leonard Lapidus, an economist, who shares her enthusiasm for Chinese food. They live in New York City.